D1084033

Public Personnel Management

Jay M. Shafritz
foreword by
Dale S. Beach

The Praeger Special Studies program—utilizing the most modern and efficient book production techniques and a selective worldwide distribution network—makes available to the academic, government, and business communities significant, timely research in U.S. and international economic, social, and political development.

CE

Public Personnel Management
The Heritage of Civil Service Reform

PRAEGER SPECIAL STUDIES IN U.S. ECONOMIC, SOCIAL, AND POLITICAL ISSUES

Praeger Publishers   New York   Washington   London

008757

Library of Congress Cataloging in Publication Data

Shafritz, Jay M
    Public personnel management.

    (Praeger special studies in U.S. economic, social,
and political issues)
    Bibliography: p.
    Includes index.
    1. Civil service—United States.   I.   Title.
JK765.S453   1975   353.001   74-31508
ISBN 0-275-05840-9

PRAEGER PUBLISHERS
111 Fourth Avenue, New York, N.Y. 10003, U.S.A.

Published in the United States of America in 1975
by Praeger Publishers, Inc.

Printed in the United States of America

Jay M. Shafritz has written a very stimulating and deliberately provocative book about the practice of public personnel administration. Many who are active in this field, whether as practitioners in government, consultants, or professors in universities, may react defensively and negatively to the charges made by the author. However, if they ignore or reject Shafritz' message, they may well have misunderstood his central thesis. He is issuing a clarion call to uplift the sights and change the focus of the public personnel field.

The author knows whereof he speaks. He has been intimately involved in public personnel management at both the municipal and federal level. His argument in this treatise is impressively supported and documented. He displays a keen ability to grasp the essential meaning and implications of the entire civil service reform movement and of contemporary personnel administration in government service.

The civil service reform movement arose out of legitimate needs to correct the evils of the spoils system and to improve and stabilize performance in government agencies and bureaus. In working toward this goal, however, excessive bureaucratic rigidities have been introduced and institutionalized. Personnel specialists have succumbed to "goal displacement." They have become so enamored with administering employment examinations, analyzing and classifying jobs, and designing performance rating plans (that is, the procedural control functions of personnel) that they have lost sight of the fact that agency mission, efficiency, and high performance are important goals. Indeed, a potentially exciting challenge to public personnel management can be the creation and operation of soundly based programs to improve both productivity and job satisfaction in the public service. Such a change of focus will require new vision and broader goals. Education and preparation for careers in the field will have to be changed. Public personnel management can and should become more professionalized.

A golden opportunity exists for the public personnel field to change from a preoccupation with organizational maintenance to an emphasis upon system improvement and innovation. Shafritz proposes position management as the

vehicle for system improvement through the optimal development and utilization of human resources. By setting up
task forces with personnel specialists as facilitators,
the work of the organization can be redesigned to provide
motivation through the work itself and to provide for personal growth, advancement, recognition, and self-responsi-
bility. If combined with organization development--Shaf-
ritz mentions OD but does not accord it a major role--job
redesign and enrichment can become major mechanisms for
total system improvement and human resource development.

Powerful external forces are operating today to bring
about an expansion and uplifting of the role of public personnel management. One of these forces is the law regarding
equal employment opportunity. It is shocking to acknowledge that thousands upon thousands of civil service tests
(for hiring and promotion) have been administered over the
years without the vast majority of these ever having been
validated empirically. Equal Employment Opportunity Commission and court rulings are now forcing more soundly
based practices. Another force for change is the spread
of unionization and collective bargaining in public employment. Whereas the full implications of this trend are
yet to be perceived, one can expect greater emphasis upon
human resource development, more employee participation
through joint committees, and more power equalization in
the bureaucracy. (Some perhaps would say that power equalization in a bureaucracy is an anachronism.)

I commend this book to all serious students and professionals in public administration. Many will agree with
Shafritz' propositions, many will vigorously challenge his
views, but none can reasonably ignore them.

ACKNOWLEDGMENTS

This book would not have been written without the initial encouragement that I received from the National Civil Service League. I am much indebted to Jean L. Couturier, Executive Director of the NCSL and his associate directors, Ada Kimsey and Bruce Petty. Many individuals helped me with the preparation of the manuscript by reading portions of it, discussing and challenging many of the ideas contained herein, and leading me to source material. Some of them are: Fred Arend, Anna Auletta, James Curvey, and Paul Long of the HUD Office of Personnel; Robert Fagan of the Executive Development Program of the Department of Labor; Norman Powell of Baruch College; Seymour Berlin of the American Society for Public Administration; Frederick Mosher of the University of Virginia; Vincent Marando of the University of Georgia; and Daniel Oran of the Antioch College School of Law. My mentioning them here in no way implies that they approve of or even have foreknowledge of all the material that follows.

Rensselaer Polytechnic Institute has been most understanding in allowing me the necessary time to write. Special thanks to Dean Harry Smith of the School of Management and Dean Thomas Phelan of the School of Humanities and Social Sciences. Other RPI colleagues were also kind enough to assist me. I am indebted to Professors Dale Beach, Harold Brazil, Joseph Brown, Ronald Calinger, Frank Steggert, and William Wallace.

Earlier drafts of two of the chapters have appeared elsewhere. Chapter 4, "Position Management: A Conceptual Framework for Personnel Administration," originally appeared in the Spring 1973 issue of Good Government, the journal of the National Civil Service League. It was co-authored by Bruce Petty. Chapter 7, "Political Culture: The Determinant of Merit System Viability," originally appeared in the January/February 1974 issue of Public Personnel Management, the journal of the International Personnel Management Association. Both articles have been thoroughly revised and doubled in size for this presentation.

My greatest debt is to my wife, Luise, who not only typed the various drafts of the manuscript but also added immensely to the clarity of the book by refusing to type many a tangled sentence until I translated it into English prose. And lastly, special thanks to Todd Jonathan Alexander for his invariably sound editorial judgments.

For any errors of judgment or of fact, I am solely responsible.

CONTENTS

Public Personnel Management

Consider the following:

An internal study of the New York City government found that the civil service system was an inadequate, outdated, rigid, and largely "meritless" bureaucracy that "seems to discriminate against the most qualified applicants for the public service."[1]

The former police chief of New Haven, James F. Ahearn, has stated that the civil service promotion system was "a cover for the very manipulations it was supposed to eliminate. It functioned perfectly to make the public think that the system was objective and shielded the behind-the-scenes machinations of politicians and crooks."[2]

While almost all of Chicago's municipal employees have civil service status, it is estimated that about 40 percent of them are classified as "temporaries," which means that they obtained appointments without undergoing formal examining procedures and may remain in such jobs for no more than 180 days. "Some politically active employees have held these 180-day temporary jobs for twenty years."[3]

Applicants for new positions as well as for promotions in the federal service have been "asked flatly by bosses whether they were registered Republicans or Democrats."[4] The U.S. Civil Service Commission has begun a formal investigation into charges that at least one federal department has been violating the law by appointing political favorites to career civil service positions.[5] The executive director of the U.S. Civil Service Commission, Bernard Rosen, has publicly admitted that officials have been "breaking the law" with regard to their hiring practices.[6]

The conditions depicted in the jurisdictions mentioned above are not unusual. The perversion of most civil

1

service merit systems for private, administrative, and especially partisan ends is one of the worst kept, yet least
written about, secrets in government. While the general
textbooks on state and local government frequently recognize this situation,[7] the specialized texts on public personnel administration tend to deal with this subject as if
it were an abnormal malignancy instead of an inherent and
frequently beneficial part of governmental personnel management. This is faulty perspective. Just as corruption
has long been recognized as "a normal condition of American local government,"[8] so it must be recognized that the
perversion of merit system principles is a normal condition of the public personnel process. The latter situation
is not necessarily as unhealthy and undesirable as the former. Frequently such "perversions" are essential if actual
merit is to be rewarded within the "merit" system. Unfortunately, other considerations seem just as likely to apply.

     Throughout the United States, public personnel merit
systems tend to operate on two different planes within the
same jurisdiction. The great majority of civil service
employees within merit systems are able to enter and advance on the basis of their own talents and the design of
the system. However, at the same time and within the same
system there are two groups of individuals entering and
advancing according to criteria other than those provided
for by the merit system regulations.

     This first group of employees consists of all those
who were appointed for considerations other than personal
fitness. Here are hidden the political appointees in ex-
cess of those policy-making and confidential positions
that are usually the executive's prerogative. These positions are only obtained through months of diligent effort
--seeking to elect or re-elect the chief executive officer
--or through other appropriate sponsorship. Mike Causey,
a Washington Post columnist, aptly states that both the
White House and the Congress "all too often defend the
career civil service system up to the point where a friend
or brother-in-law needs a job badly."[9] The same can be
said of governors and state legislatures, of mayors and
city councils. It is a time-honored practice for a limited
number of such politicos to be fudged into presumably merit
system positions. The extent of such placements depends
upon such factors as the strength and longevity of the
merit system, the political culture of the community, and
the integrity of the executive who, having taken an oath
to uphold all the laws of his jurisdiction, can only make
such appointments in violation of the spirit, if not the

letter, of his oath. Such patronage appointments are well
known for their not totally undeserved reputation for low
productivity as well as for souring the morale of the more
conscientious employees. For example, in Philadelphia,
where Frank L. Rizzo is the mayor, it seems that the municipal revenue commissioner resigned "because he couldn't
get 191 Rizzo patronage employees to do any work and Rizzo
wouldn't let him replace them with patronage employees who
would work."[10]

While the merit system is frequently perverted for
traditional political ends, it is similarly abused for
more scrupulous purposes. The excessively rigid procedures
for entering and advancing in most merit systems have long
been recognized as being hindrances to effective management practices. A variety of good government groups have
joined political executives in condemning such regressive
practices.[11] In order to compensate for the lack of managerial discretion occasioned by such rigidities, career
civil servants as well as other highly qualified individuals
have either been advanced or initially installed through a
fudging of the civil service regulations similar to the
process by which politicos are employed. The merit system
with its procedural morass simply does not allow for the
timely placement of such meritorious individuals. What
frequently exists in fact, although nowhere is it officially
recognized, is a first-class and second-class civil service.
This is not a reflection on the quality of the individual
or of the productive value of each class; it is merely a
reference to how people are treated by the merit system.
While those comprising the civil service proletariat must
be content with careers bounded by the full force of the
frequently unreasonable and always constraining regulations,
others--fortunate enough to be recognized for their talents or in spite of their talents--benefit markedly by having these same regulations waived, fraudulently complied
with, or simply ignored. The reader should take care not
to judge such activities until he or she is fully aware
of the circumstances that have encouraged this double standard to develop. A major theme of this book is to frame
such merit system machinations within a proper perspective.

There is much wisdom in Up the Organization, the best
seller of a few years back by Robert Townsend, the man who
made the Avis Rent-a-Car Company "try harder." Although
it is spiced with humor, the book offers much serious and
valuable advice to managers. Townsend establishes his
credentials as an administrative analyst, for this reader
at least, when he recommends as an efficiency move a sim-

ple expedient, "fire the whole personnel department,"[12] the functions previously performed by personnel henceforth to be undertaken by one of the brighter secretaries. When you consider what most public personnel units actually do for their organizations, the good sense of this idea becomes immediately apparent. Since in most public organizations the negative or policing role of the personnel operation tends to be dominant, contributions to positive management are usually minimal. Consequently, from a strictly internal management viewpoint, the loss of such an internal watchdog or gadfly would seem to have a beneficial effect, since the personnel unit's positive functions could easily be reallocated to line agencies. In addition, substantial savings could be had by eliminating most of the reasons for the personnel unit's operating budget. But such a reorganization is not only improbable, it would also be illegal. Public personnel management, deriving its authority and justification from constitutional and legislative mandates, has a set of operating premises that are different from corresponding units in the private sector. What may be feasible in a private company becomes an entirely different matter when a similar application is sought in a public bureaucracy. Not following Townsend's recommendation may be wasteful; nevertheless, it is public policy that governmental personnel programs be run in a manner frequently inconsistent with efficient management practices.

Peter Drucker, one of the most renowned and influential management thinkers, offers an explanation for this seeming irrationality. Drucker maintains that government is an inherently poor manager because it is, of necessity, obsessed by procedure in order to establish accountability. The merit system apparatus of position classifications, examinations, and certification procedures grew up in direct response to previous abuses. Since individuals once showed themselves incapable of being responsible for equitable personnel operations, discretion over these matters was taken out of their hands and given to unemotional, unbending, and, in some circumstances, irrational classification, examination, and certification procedures. Accountability was placed in procedures rather than in individuals, the rationale being that the honest administration of the public's business was too important a matter to leave to an individual's discretion. It is precisely because governmental and especially public personnel procedures attempt to assign accountability for everything that public management operations grow to be outrageously expensive when compared to similar functions in private industry.

4

According to Drucker, government must always tolerate this extra expense--not out of some unwarranted affection for red tape, but because a "little dishonesty" in government is a corrosive disease that rapidly spreads to infect the entire polity. To fear such corruption is quite rational. Consequently, government "bureaucracy" and its attendant high costs cannot and should not be eliminated.[13]

While the high costs of accountability can never be totally eliminated, some of the dysfunctions of associated procedures can be mitigated. Such mitigation frequently has the personnel agency bending, ignoring, and subverting the civil service regulations in the interests of good management. The discretion that the regulations deny to the public executive is restored to him by the machinations of his personnel operatives. When the flexibility deemed essential for mission accomplishment is formally denied to line managers, it is almost invariably obtained informally through administrative finesse. This is an idea that has not only been demonstrated in countless empirical studies,[14] but also is sanctioned and revered in American popular culture. As a nation we have a tremendous appetite for movies and television programs about war and other violent escapades. As any aficionado with sufficient exposure to this this genre of entertainment can explain, you cannot have a successful military operation without a scrounger in your unit--at least not according to Hollywood's version of World War II. A scrounger was that member of the team assigned to obtain all the essential requirements of the mission that could not be obtained through official channels. It hardly mattered what methods the scroungers used to secure the needed supplies as long as they succeeded, and there were no official complaints. Undoubtedly the war was won because our scroungers were better than their scroungers. The Germans, having invented bureaucracy, perhaps felt themselves more bound by its constraints.

While there is no truth to the rumor that all the scroungers of World War II became public personnel officers during the postwar period, it is true that the scrounger mentality is pervasive in American public bureaucracies. Scrounger philosophy is essentially Machiavellian--the end justifies the means. The end may be the execution of a public policy that is both innovative and noble in scope; the means is frequently the assembling of a staff that is capable of achieving such grand designs. To the extent that civil service rules and regulations do not facilitate such an assembly, the personnel officer or staff must scrounge to get them. The task is not so much one of locating ap-

propriate talent as it is one of bringing that talent into
the organization. Line managers, being the mission-oriented
officers that they are, tend to exhibit a wanton disregard
for the means--ethical and otherwise--by which their personnel resources are obtained. A personnel officer is
judged by his ability to produce results--not by his lucid
explanations of why the civil service regulations make it
impossible to hire this person or to promote that one.

The obvious danger of managers using excessive zeal
in seeking to achieve their agency's mission, and thereby
going beyond the proper range of their discretion, is well
recognized. This is an inherent and necessary risk in all
managerial delegation. Unreasonable constraints only exac-
erbate the danger and increase the frustration. When legislative mandates that reflect neither administrative wisdom
nor experience are viewed as barriers to managerial effectiveness, they tend to intensify the "bureaucratic search
for modes of action functional in removing, circumventing,
or otherwise mastering the barrier."[15] There is even significant evidence that organizational superiors discourage
subordinates from fully reporting just how they have accomplished their missions because of concerns for legal
culpability. As Herbert Kaufman has observed, executives
in public agencies "may resort to the strategy of discour-
aging feedback about administrative behavior because they
privately approve of the behavior they know they should,
according to law and morality, prevent."[16]

While there is certainly nothing new about discussing
the informal aspects of administrative behavior, analyses
of bureaucratic realpolitik have long been conspicuously
lacking.[17] Just as rookie policemen are told by their more
experienced associates that they will have to forget everything they learned at the police academy before they can
effectively operate in a real world situation,[18] a new public manager, whether he has a liberal arts background or a
master's in public administration, must suffer through an
on-the-job acquisition of administrative realpolitik.
"He learns by the punishing effects of violating norms
whose existence and whose particular application he dis-
covers by their breach."[19] This seems an unnecessary and
gratuitous bit of trauma to impose upon innocent individuals. Accordingly the intent of this book is to help ease
this loss of administrative innocence as well as to examine
the origins, present manifestations, and possible resolution of the double-standard merit system and its attendant
scroungers. This double standard, with its associated bureaucratic tendencies, is the bittersweet heritage of civil
service reform.

NOTES

1. New York _Times_, November 16, 1972, p. 1.

2. New York _Times_, April 16, 1972, p. 52.

3. Martin and Susan Tolchin, _To the Victor: Political Patronage from the Clubhouse to the White House_ (New York: Vintage Books, 1972), pp. 40-41.

4. Reported by Mike Causey in the Washington _Post_, May 4, 1973, p. D17.

5. New York _Times_, November 11, 1973, p. 1.

6. Reported by Mike Causey in the Washington _Post_, December 3, 1973, p. B13.

7. Typically, they have concluded that "personnel officers who, while rendering lip service to the merit principle, are spoilsmen at heart, can find innumberable ways of circumventing statutory requirements." Clyde F. Snider, _American State and Local Government_, 2d ed. (New York: Appleton-Century-Crofts, 1965), pp. 298-99. For an expression of similar sentiments, see York Willbern, "Personnel and Money," in James W. Fesler, ed., _The 50 States and Their Local Governments_ (New York: Knopf, 1967), pp. 374-75.

8. Daniel P. Moynihan, "The Private Government of Organized Crime," _Reporter_ 25 (July 16, 1961): 14.

9. Washington _Post_, January 9, 1974, p. B13.

10. Joseph R. Daughen, "Rizzo in 1973: Defeat and Painful Political Education," Philadelphia _Bulletin_, December 31, 1973, p. B3.

11. For statements deploring merit system rigidities by the National League of Cities and the U.S. Conference of Mayors, see Michael A. DiNunzio and Nancy Hall, "Manning Tomorrow's Cities: In Search of Professionals," _Nation's Cities_ 11 (June 1973): 40. For a similar statement by the National Civil Service League, see Jean J. Couturier, "Civil Service Reform--1970s Style," _Good Government_ 90 (Summer 1973): 18.

12. Robert Townsend, _Up the Organization: How to Stop the Corporation from Stifling People and Strangling Profits_ (Greenwich, Conn.: Fawcett, 1970), p. 126.

13. Peter F. Drucker, "The Sickness of Government," _Public Interest_ 14 (Winter 1969): 15.

14. For summaries of this data, see Keith Davis, _Human Behavior at Work: Human Relations and Organizational Behavior_, 4th ed. (New York: McGraw-Hill, 1972), pp. 251-73; Amitai Etzioni, _Modern Organizations_ (Englewood Cliffs, N.J.: Prentice-Hall, 1964), pp. 40-49; Herbert G. Hicks, _The Management of Organizations: A Systems and Human Re-

sources Approach, 2d ed. (New York: McGraw-Hill, 1972), pp. 14-16; Daniel Katz and Robert L. Kahn, The Social Psychology of Organizations (New York: Wiley, 1966), pp. 80-81.

15. Husain Mustafa and Anthony A. Salomone, "Administrative Circumvention of Public Policy," Midwest Review of Public Administration 5, no. 1 (1971): 17. Administrative circumvention is also discussed by Paul Appleby, Policy and Administration (University: University of Alabama Press, 1949), p. 47.

16. Herbert Kaufman, Administrative Feedback: Monitoring Subordinates' Behavior (Washington, D.C.: Brookings Institution, 1973), p. 65.

17. "Scanning the literature of American public administration, anyone familiar with the realities of bureaucratic existence is struck by the almost total absence of any dispassionate analysis of the nature and importance of administrative realpolitik." Albert Somit, "Bureaucratic Realpolitik and the Teaching of Administration," in Claude E. Hawley and Ruth G. Weintraub, eds., Administrative Questions and Political Answers (Princeton, N.J.: D. Van Nostrand, 1966), p. 540. While Somit originally published this article in 1956, his statement remains substantially valid today.

18. Arthur Niederhoffer, Behind the Shield: The Police in Urban Society (Garden City, N.Y.: Doubleday Anchor, 1969), p. 47.

19. Norton E. Long, "The Administration Organization as a Political System," in Sidney Mailick and Edward H. Van Ness, eds., Concepts and Issues in Administrative Behavior (Englewood Cliffs, N.J.: Prentice-Hall, 1962), p. 142.

2

THE CIVIL
SERVICE REFORM
MOVEMENT

A HISTORICAL PERSPECTIVE

An unfortunate characteristic of triteness is its frequent veracity. Thus, it may come as no surprise to the
reader that public personnel management is in a time of
transition. It was ever so. When the first major textbook was published on this subject in 1936, the authors
were able to state with great justification that "thorough-
going reform of personnel administration is long overdue."[1]
This statement is equally true today, but with a crucial
difference. While the early reform efforts concentrated
upon creating institutions, the thrust of present-day efforts is centered upon reforming institutions. It is a
vexing philosophical question as to which reform effort
is the more difficult undertaking. Transitions must be
viewed widely--historically. They cannot be understood
simply within the confines of the present. An examination
of the past is the key not only to the present but to the
future as well. Just as an individual's life cannot be appreciated properly without reviewing the time of childhood
and youth, the modern import of a social movement, in this
case civil service reform, cannot be appreciated without
reviewing the hopes of its founders, the environment that
molded it, and its evolution over time.

Time tends to sanctify, and few governmental practices
have developed such airs of sanctity as have civil service
procedures. Freedom from such false sanctification, from
unreasoning tradition, comes with exposure. Only after
the origins of the various civil service rituals are in
perspective can the basic doctrines be revised to accommodate a modern world. However, the debunking of the false

icons of the merit system must be approached with mixed
feelings. While its sundry rituals may have grown unre-
sponsive to present-day needs, its moral underpinnings,
hypocrisy notwithstanding, are still crucial for the viability and legitimacy of our public institutions. Separa-
ting the ritual from the philosophy is a delicate undertaking. Yet it must be done, for the underlying philosophy
and moral impetus of the civil service reform movement has
remained valid while its ritual has grown dysfunctional.
The history and analysis that follows is necessarily abbre-
viated. Its purpose is simply to lay out all the main
threads of the past that still have a pull on the present.
For only then can the problems of today be faced with a
sense of place, a sense of proportion, and a sense of humor.

While a civil service has long been a feature of government, a career civil service based upon merit has until
comparatively recently been a historical novelty. Such
corps have popped in and out of history since the days of
ancient China,[2] but merit systems in the modern sense had
to await the advent of industrialization and the modern
nation-state. Prussia, one of the constituent states of
what was to become modern Germany, was the first modern
nation to institute a merit system.[3] It was this German
civil service that inspired Max Weber's famous "ideal-type"
bureaucratic model that is the point of departure for all
present-day discussions of bureaucratic theory.[4] Weber,
a scholar of prodigious output, is considered to be one of
the principal founders of the academic discipline of public
administration.[5] Prussia began its merit system in the
mid-18th century. France followed the Prussian model
shortly after the revolution of 1789. Great Britain, after
developing a professionalized civil service for India in
the 1830s, adopted the concept for the homeland in the
1850s. The United States was among the last of the major
industrialized nations to inaugurate a civil service based
on merit.

Depending upon your point of view, the advent of modern merit systems is either an economic, political, or a
moral development. Economic historians would maintain that
the demands of industrial expansion, that is, a dependable
postal service, a viable transportation network, and so
on, necessitated a government service based upon merit.
Political analysts could argue persuasively that it was
the demands of an expanded suffrage and democratic rhetoric
that sought to replace favoritism with merit. While Weber
has sided with the economic view, economic and political
considerations are so intertwined that it is impossible to

say what factor is the true midwife of the merit system. The moral impetus behind reform is even more difficult to divine. As moral impulses tend to hide economic and political motives, the weight of moral concern that is undiluted by other considerations is impossible to measure. Nevertheless, the cosmetic effect of moral overtones was of significant aid to the civil service reform movement in the United States because it accented the social legitimacy of the reform proposals.

Since a primary aim of this book is to diagnose the condition of the American public service of today, it is essential to seek the roots of any possible malignancies in the history of the reform movement. While civil service reform is generally dated from the post-Civil War period, the political roots of the reform effort go back much earlier--to the beginning of the republic. As John Adams tended to maintain the appointments of George Washington, Thomas Jefferson was the first president who had to face the problem of a philosophically hostile bureaucracy. While sorely pressed by his supporters to remove Federalist officeholders and replace them with Republican partisans, Jefferson was determined not to remove officials for political reasons alone. Jefferson rather courageously maintained that only "malconduct is a just ground of removal: mere difference of political opinion is not."[6] With occasional defections from this principle, even by Jefferson himself,[7] this policy was the norm rather than the exception down through the administration of Andrew Jackson.

THE JACKSONIAN LEGACY

Poor Andrew Jackson has been blamed for inventing the spoils system. Many a high school student will tell you that upon becoming president Jackson shouted, "To the victor belong the spoils," and thereupon fired everybody in the government and replaced them with incompetent friends. But the truth is much more subtle. Far from firing everybody, Jackson continued with the appointing practices established by his predecessors. The federal service before Jackson's administration was a stable, long-tenured corps of faithful officials decidedly elitist in character and remarkably barren of corruption. Jackson for the most part continued with this tradition in practice.[8] He turned out of office about as many appointees as had Jefferson. During his eight years in office (1829-37) removals are generally estimated to have been less than 20 percent.[9]

Yet popular historians and, no doubt, high school teachers are still maintaining that "it is a fair statement that Jackson introduced the spoils system into the federal government."[10] If it was spoils, it was of a much milder variety than was to flourish in succeeding administrations when the turnover rate was likely to be an overwhelming majority of the civil service. As for that famous phrase, "to the victor belong the spoils," it was neither uttered by Jackson nor recorded at all until the latter part of Jackson's first term as president. The famous phrase maker was Senator William L. Marcy of New York, who, in an 1832 debate with Senator Henry Clay of Kentucky over Jackson's nomination of Martin Van Buren as Minister to Great Britain, stated that the politicians of the United States "see nothing wrong in the rule that to the victor belong the spoils of the enemy."[11] Marcy was to get his comeuppance years later when, as secretary of state under President Pierce, he futilely sought to establish the rudiments of a career system for clerks in the State Department.[12]

The changes that Jackson made in the civil service must be interpreted as those of a reformer anxious to see the civil service more representative of its national constituency, as well as those of a party leader anxious to pay off political debts. Jackson merely wanted to reform the civil service in this rather limited aspect; he was not inclined to alter its nature radically. As he tended to pursue the personnel policies of his predecessors, his rhetoric on the nature of the public service was to be far more influential than his administrative example. To appreciate fully the historical place of Jackson's civil service ideology, one must be aware of several environmental influences. While there was general agreement at the time that the civil service represented a high degree of competence and integrity, there was also widespread resentment that appointments still tended to go to members of families of social standing at a time when universal white male suffrage had finally become a reality. To a large degree Jackson's constituency was made up of the previously disenfranchised and their sympathizers.[13] In this context Jackson's famous attack upon what had become an elitist and inbred civil service was well justified. That attack, which is also the most famous defense of what was to become the spoils system, came with his first annual message to Congress in December 1829. Jackson's eloquence on the inevitable insensitivity to the public interest caused by excessive tenure in public office is as valid and prophetic today as it was then.

There are, perhaps, few men who can for any
great length of time enjoy office and power without being more or less under the influence of
feelings unfavorable to the faithful discharge of
their public duties. Their integrity may be proof
against improper considerations immediately addressed to themselves, but they are apt to acquire
a habit of looking with indifference upon the public interests and of tolerating conduct from which
an unpracticed man would revolt. Office is considered as a species of property, and government
rather as a means of promoting individual interests than as an instrument created solely for the
service of the people. Corruption in some and in
others a perversion of correct feelings and principles divert government from its legitimate ends
and make it an engine for the support of the few
at the expense of the many.[14]

How ironic that the original intent of this philosophic
justification of the spoils system, which was to become
synonymous with the corruption of public office, was to
limit the tendency toward corruption occasioned by long
tenure in office! The analogy that Jackson makes to public office being "considered as a species of property" was
unwittingly resurrected by Norman Mailer's analysis of the
Democratic and Republican national conventions of 1968,
Miami and the Siege of Chicago. In assuming that "politics
is property," Mailer reiterates Jackson's view that public
office is all too frequently used as a means to promote individual interests to the violation of the public's trust
and the detriment of the public interest.[15]

In this same message Jackson went on to make his most
famous statement on the character of public office:

The duties of all public officers are, or at least
admit of being made, so plain and simple that men
of intelligence may readily qualify themselves for
their performance; and I cannot but believe that
more is lost by the long continuance of men in office than is generally to be gained by their experience.[16]

In the context of the times, Jackson was asserting that
all men--not just the aristocratic elite and the property
owners, but the newly enfranchised common men that did so
much to elect Jackson--should have an equal opportunity

for public office. Jackson went on to say that "in a country where offices are created solely for the benefit of the people no one man has any more intrinsic right to official station than another."[17] In playing to his plebeian constituency, Jackson put the patrician civil service on notice that they had no natural monopoly on public office. "The doctrine of rotation in office was thus in large part conceived as a sincere measure of reform."[18] As such, this notion was enthusiastically supported by many of the professional reformers of the day.[19] But presidential rhetoric, then as now, frequently has little relation to presidential actions. As demonstrated by Sidney H. Aronson, Jackson's appointments were as elitist in nature as the appointments of his predecessors Adams and Jefferson.[20] While Jackson's personal indulgence in spoils was more limited than commonly thought, he did establish the intellectual and political rationale for the unmitigated spoils system that was to follow. With his simple eloquence, "the doctrine of spoils was endowed with the dignity of a political theory most appealing to American democratic sensibilities."[21] Of course, Jackson's spoils doctrine took hold as it did because the country was well prepared to accept it. Indeed, much of the venality of the spoils process was in full flower in many state and local governments a full generation before it crept into federal office.[22]

A nagging question remains. If Jackson's indulgence in spoils was so very limited, why has Jackson become its symbol?[23]

> Jackson's opponents wielded every resource at their command in an attempt to discredit the new administration and its policy of "reform." The spoils system was still novel enough in American national politics that its introduction and encouragement sparked violent controversy--controversy further fanned by executive-legislative as well as personal antagonisms. Magnified by word of mouth, blared forth in the press, and exaggerated in the heat of political conflict, the Jacksonian readjustment of the public service soon became the American symbol of political partisanship, while the famous phrase of Senator Marcy became its slogan.[24]

Jackson's rhetoric notwithstanding, the spoils system did not come into full flower until a decade later. Martin Van Buren, who succeeded Jackson in 1837, continued with a moderate view of removals until the latter part of his term when his unsuccessful campaign for re-election demanded a more partisan strategy. With a new party in the White House in 1840, spoils appointments became the norm rather than the exception. President William Henry Harrison, "Old Tippecanoe," had a short term of office. He caught pneumonia during his second week as president and died during the third. However, his vice-president, John Tyler, gave the spoils full bipartisan support and assured its permanence on the national scene. The doctrine of rotation of office progressively prevailed over the earlier notion of stability in office. Presidents even began turning out of office appointees of previous presidents of the same party. President Millard Fillmore had dissident Whigs turned out in favor of "real" Whigs.[25] When James Buchanan, a Democrat, succeeded Franklin Pierce, also a Democrat, it was announced that no incumbents appointed by Pierce would be retained. This development led William Marcy to remark, "They have it that I am the author of the office seeker's doctrine, that 'to the victors belong the spoils,' but I certainly should never recommend the policy of pillaging my own camp."[26] Lincoln as president followed the example of his predecessors and was an unabashed supporter and skillful user of the spoils system.[27]

As opposed to the frequent historical view that Lincoln's problems with "jobseekers constituted a serious interference with the prosecution of the Civil War,"[28] more responsible historians take the view that had it not been for Lincoln's highly partisan exploitation of federal patronage, the Civil War could not have been won—at least not by the North.[29] Paradoxically, while the spoils system reached its zenith under Lincoln, its decline may also be dated from his administration; for Lincoln refused to accede to the hitherto observed principle of quadrennial rotation after his re-election in 1864.[30] This was the first significant setback that the principle of rotation had received since Jackson laid out its theoretical justifications in 1829.

Yet through all this, the height of the spoils period, there existed what Leonard White has called a "career service."[31] Many clerks had continuous tenure all through this period, retaining their positions because of competence, custom, and neutrality. Assuming that the historians are correct as to the general incompetence and indolence of the spoils appointees of the time, these career clerks were apparently the ones who did most of the work of the government. Somebody had to have done it.

While the modern civil service reform movement did not begin until after the Civil War, there was one successful effort during the 1850s to implement a system of civil service examinations before this time. In an age when basic literacy was by no means universal, it occurred to some congressmen that even with political considerations paramount in the appointing process, some effort should be made to determine if those assuming clerical positions had the most rudimentary skills. The military had since 1814 required examinations to determine the competence of potential surgeons. Over the next few decades, examinations were made mandatory for a variety of officer positions.[32] While some members of Congress sought to have the military example emulated by the departmental clerks as early as 1842,[33] it was not until 1853 that Congress authorized the installation of a system of qualifying examinations for a portion of the departmental clerks. The examinations, conducted by the appointing departments themselves, merely sought to establish minimum standards and had no other influence upon the appointing process. This same legislation established the rudiments of a position classification program by arranging clerks into four classes based upon salary.[34] While these measures mitigated to the smallest degree the effect of spoils upon the federal administration, there was no such mitigation at the state and local level.

THE IMPETUS FOR REFORM

Nothing so complicated as the civil service reform movement can be explained simply, if only because altruistic motives were so inexorably mingled with self-interest. In reviewing the distinct strains of influence upon the reform effort, one finds little purity. Yet for the purposes of analysis it is possible to identify four mutually supportive factors that jointly made reform a reality and established the basic character of our present public ser-

vice: the quest for political power by the "out" group;
social class antagonisms; moral indignation; and an expanding industrialization. Each will be considered in turn.

It was congressional disenchantment with the policies
of President Andrew Johnson that instigated the first comprehensive and highly publicized proposals for a merit system based upon competitive examinations. Congressman Thomas
A. Jenckes, a Republican of Rhode Island, sponsored several
bills to curb the patronage power of the president by
foisting a merit system upon him. Jenckes' proposals,
which borrowed heavily from the British model, were worthy
in and of themselves; but they were obviously inspired, at
least initially, by antipathy to President Johnson.[35]
While Jenckes' 1865 proposals advocated a civil service
commission appointed by the president, a growing hostility
toward President Johnson certainly motivated the strikingly
novel feature of his 1868 proposals: "to furnish employment for the Vice-President by making him the head of a
new department--that of the civil service."[36] This was a
thinly disguised effort to take patronage out of the hands
of a president whose appointments tended to antagonize the
Congress. Once Johnson was out of office, Jenckes reverted
to his original proposal for a presidentially appointed
commission to administer a civil service merit system.[37]
But the Jenckes proposals, having to compete for public
attention with Andrew Johnson's impeachment trial and the
forthcoming Republican National Convention, made little impact. Johnson's impeachment was occasioned by his violation of the Tenure of Office Act of 1867. Many of the nation's opinion leaders of the time, including the Nation
and the New York Times, praised the act as a sincere measure of reform that would bring stability to the government
service.[38] Since the whole impeachment controversy can be
viewed from one perspective as a struggle between the executive and the legislative branches for the control of patronage, the Jenckes proposal to have the vice-president
serve as a buffer between the president and the Congress
does not seem so outlandish considering the time frame.

While the various reform proposals that Jenckes put
forth during the Johnson administration owed their origins
to mixed motives on the congressman's part, they did, nevertheless, serve as an important rallying point for reform
agitation. The movers and shakers of the budding reform
movement as well as many of the important newspapers and
journals of the day gave the Jenckes proposals considerable attention. The civil service reform movement that
eventually led to the Pendleton Act did not exist in 1866.

Jenckes' initial reform proposals of 1865 and 1866 were literally ignored by the press and other national opinion leaders. Yet within five years the reform movement had mobilized to the extent that the President of the United States, Ulysses S. Grant, recommended civil service legislation to the Congress in 1870 and obtained it in 1871. Jenckes deserves considerable credit for this mobilization of opinion and attention. However, possibly because he did not pay enough attention to his own patronage garden, Jenckes was defeated for re-election in 1970, and he retired from public life.[39]

In 1859, Ulysses S. Grant, as a private and obscure citizen, sought an appointment as a county engineer in Missouri and was denied it because he lacked the requisite political sponsorship.[40] This may have inspired Grant's support for civil service reform when he became president. It is one of the cruelties of one-dimensional popular history that the first administration to make a large-scale effort at civil service reform should be most noted for its spoils system excesses. Reform, fleeting as it was, was achieved not after the careful and lengthy deliberations of the Congress, but mainly through the parliamentary skill of its proponents. On the last day of the legislative session of the 41st Congress in 1871, Senator Lyman Trumbull of Illinois attached to an otherwise unrelated appropriations bills a rider authorizing the president to make rules and regulations for the civil service. Surprisingly, the total bill was approved by both houses, though not without difficulty. While Grant supported the measure, historians tend to argue that the bill passed not because of Grant's influence but because of an awakening public opinion that had been coalescing for several years around the Jenckes proposals.[41] Contributing to this arousal were the recent exposés of Boss Tweed's operations in New York City and other journalistic ferment.[42] The rider itself was only one sentence long and did not formally require the president to do anything. It certainly would not have passed had it been thought to be anything more than a symbolic sop to the reformers. The rider states:

> That the President of the United States be, and he is hereby, authorized to prescribe such rules and regulations for the admission of persons into the civil service of the United States as will best promote the efficiency thereof, and ascertain the fitness of each candidate in respect to

age, health, character, knowledge, and ability for the branch of service into which he seeks to enter; and for this purpose the President is authorized to employ suitable persons to conduct said inquiries, to prescribe their duties, and to establish regulations for the conduct of persons who may receive appointments in the civil service.[43]

To the surprise of almost everyone, Grant proceeded to appoint a civil service commission on the very next day.[44] He authorized them to establish and implement appropriate rules and regulations. The chairman of the commission was George William Curtis, editor of <u>Harper's Weekly</u> and one of the leaders of the reform movement.[45] The commission required boards of examiners in each department who administered their program under the commission's general supervision. All things considered, a viable program existed during 1872 and 1873. Several thousand persons were examined and several hundred were actually appointed. But once the Congress realized that Grant was serious about reform and intent upon cutting into their patronage powers, the program was terminated. Congress simply refused to appropriate funds for the work of the commission. While the president formally abolished his commission in 1875, the enabling legislation, the rider of 1871, remains law to this day.[46]

While the first Federal Civil Service Commission was short-lived, the experiment served as an important object lesson for later reform measures and established presidential prerogatives that are now taken for granted. For the first time the president was given unchallengeable authority over federal government personnel. The reform measures implied by the rider went far beyond the control of personnel. By authorizing the president to, in effect, provide himself with staff assistance, the rider of 1871 marks "the beginning of the President's rise to the actual leadership of administration in the federal government."[47] It is by the authority of this rider as well as the later Pendleton Act that the president issues executive orders and rules concerning the civil service.

The policies that this first Civil Service Commission promulgated still haunt merit systems to this day. The word "haunt" in this instance seems exceedingly appropriate, for it is the dead hand of the past that is frequently keeping the public service from achieving its full potential. An analysis of the terminology and concepts developed by Grant's commission shows that many of the provisions that are taken for granted today in merit systems at all jurisdictional levels were first developed in 1871. It was this commission that first instituted the "rule of three,"[48] adopted the policy of restricting lateral entry and making initial appointments only at the entrance level,[49] and mandated that promotion within the service should be decided by competitive examinations limited to those already in the agency. It is ironic that this last measure, in such widespread use today and almost universally used in large police and fire departments, should have been found by the commission to be an unsuitable method to determine promotions.[50] All the above-mentioned measures were appropriate innovations at the time, but they have not aged well. Their practical utility is being seriously questioned today. Even the National Civil Service League is now in favor of replacing the "rule of three" with a "rule of the list" or "pass-fail" scoring system.[51] While the federal service is not generally confined by these particular constraints upon management, many state and local jurisdictions are stuck with these and similarly antiquated practices. Not only are they locked into such practices by legal mandates, tradition, and inertia; but the newly militant unions, finding that such procedures that give a decided advantage to seniority over merit are to the advantage of their members, are ever more insistent that such provisions remain.

With the demise of Grant's commission, reform took only a few halting steps until the Arthur administration. Hayes, who succeeded Grant, was personally in favor of reform, but with a Congress hostile to it, he did not press the matter beyond issuing an executive order requiring competitive examinations for the notoriously corrupt New York Custom House and for parts of the New York Post Office. His most notable act of reform was the appointment of famous reform advocate Carl Schurz as secretary of the interior. Schurz thereupon adopted a merit system for the Interior Department based upon the rules established by Grant's disbanded Civil Service Commission.

It was during the time of the Hayes administration that the various civil service reform associations were established. The first of these was the New York Civil Service Reform Association formed in 1877. By 1880 a variety of other cities had also organized associations. The National Civil Service Reform League was formed at that time "to facilitate the correspondence and the united action of the Civil Service Reform Associations."[52] These associations were to be a potent force in the fight for reform during the coming decades. It was the New York association that in 1880 drafted a reform program that was to be submitted to Congress for consideration. Meanwhile, Senator George H. Pendleton, a Democrat from Ohio, had independently and unbeknown to the association introduced a version of one of Jenckes' old proposals in the Senate. When the association learned of this, it sent Dorman B. Eaton to confer with the senator. Eaton, a prominent New York lawyer who was to become the first chairman of the present U.S. Civil Service Commission, was at the time one of the drafters of the association's reform legislative proposals. His was the delicate task of convincing the senator to replace his own bill with the one written by the association. Without such a substitution the bills would have been competing with each other and neither would have been as likely to gain eventual passage. The senator agreed to substitute the bills after being tactfully told that his original bill was both unconstitutional and impractical.[53] Thus, the "second" Pendleton bill, written by the New York Civil Service Reform Association, was submitted to the Senate on January 10, 1881. Two years later it became law.

Just as it was the assassination of President John F. Kennedy in 1963 that fostered the congressional climate essential for the passage of his previously thwarted domestic legislative goals, it was the 1881 assassination of President James A. Garfield--elected the year before on a platform calling for a complete and radical civil service reform--that created the climate necessary for the passage of the nation's first significant reform measure, the Pendleton Act of 1883. Hollywood could hardly have written a scenario that was more conducive to reform. Garfield was not shot by a mere political fanatic or run-of-the-mill deranged mind. His assassin, Charles Guiteau, was a disappointed office seeker. Guiteau, who had supported Garfield's election, had assumed that he was to receive a diplomatic post. When the president ignored his request, Guiteau was unable to deal with such frustration in a socially acceptable manner. Knowing that the vice-president, Chester A. Arthur, was such a thorough spoilsman that he was removed from his post as head of the New York Custom House by President Hayes for notorious partisan abuses, Guiteau approached Garfield at a Washington railroad station and shot him twice while shouting, "I am a stalwart and Arthur is President now."[54] Obviously, Guiteau felt that Arthur would be more receptive to his petitions for office than Garfield had been. "Though Guiteau was plainly insane, it was seen by many reasonable people that his in-

sanity differed only in degree from that of certain statesmen of the period."[55]

While popular sympathy for civil service reform was
certainly in the air, it was an idea whose time had by no
means come. But Guiteau's bitter act changed the political
climate precipitously. The reformers, who took a moralistic tone to begin with, were suddenly able to equate the
spoils system with murder. This the public took to heart.
Garfield was made a martyr to the spoils system. Sympathy
for Garfield, who dramatically took more than two months
to die as he lingered on in pain, was equated with support
for reform. Henry Adams, observing the insincere but elaborate praise that the reformers heaped upon Garfield, wrote
that "the cynical impudence with which the reformers have
tried to manufacture an ideal statesman out of the late
shady politician beats anything in novel writing."[56] The
ensuing Pendleton Act hardly provided the framework of a
modern merit system. It was essentially a gesture by, for
the most part, reluctant politicians to assuage public
opinion and the reform elements. James Bryce was to note
that civil service reform received the lip service of both
parties, "a lip service expressed by both with equal warmth
and by the average professional politician of both with
equal insincerity."[57] While Garfield's assassination was
instrumental in creating the appropriate climate for the
passage of the act, it is widely noted that the Republican
reversals during the mid-term elections of 1882 had a more
immediate effect on enactment. Civil service reform had
been the deciding issue in a number of congressional con-
tests, and the state that harbored the greatest excesses
of the spoils system, New York, elected as governor Grover
Cleveland, who was both the reform mayor from Buffalo and
a Democrat.

In addition to hurdling the substantial problems of
implementation, the civil service reform movement frequently came up against allegations that it was "un-Ameri-
can." Depending upon what aspect of reform was being discussed, it was referred to as Chinese, Prussian, or British
in origin. And so it was. The Chinese certainly had the
earliest known merit system based upon a formal system of
examinations. But if this was subversive, so was gunpow-
der--another ancient Chinese invention. Actually, the reformers made a decided point of studying the various European civil services, especially the British. At the request of President Hayes, Dorman B. Eaton, one of the most
prominent reform advocates, went to England to study the
British civil service.[58] His report was widely circulated

and even commercially published.[59] Shortly thereafter
Eaton became one of the prime drafters of the Pendleton
Act. There was considerable and well-warranted concern
that any merit system based upon the European, particularly
the British, model of having competitive examinations,
would be automatically biased in favor of college graduates.
As higher education was essentially an upper-class prerogative in the America of the last century, this was reminiscent of the aristocratic civil service that the country
found so objectionable only 50 years earlier. The examination dilemma was resolved when it was agreed, in the words
of the Pendleton Act, that "such examinations shall be
practical in their character." Presumedly this neutralized
any advantage that a college graduate might have--for in
those days there was little that was "practical" taught in
most American colleges. It was not until 1934 that the U.S.
Civil Service Commission offered its first entrance examination designed especially for liberal arts graduates.[60]
With the exception of technical and professional positions,
a decided prejudice against college graduates continued to
exist in the American public service until after World War
II.[61]

THE PENDLETON ACT

The Pendleton Act or "An Act to Regulate and Improve
the Civil Service of the United States" has been a remarkably durable piece of legislation. Within it is the framework for personnel management that is still the heart of
the federal civil service system. The act created the
present U.S. Civil Service Commission as the personnel management arm of the president. While it is termed a commission, the U.S. Civil Service Commission is by no means independent. It is an executive agency that is for all practical purposes subject to the administrative discretion of
the president. Its three commissioners, not more than two
of whom can be of the same party, serve at the pleasure of
the president. The act gave legislative legitimacy to
many of the procedures developed by the earlier unsuccessful civil service commission during the Grant administration. Written into the act were requirements for open competitive examinations, probationary periods, and protection
from political pressures. While the personnel program was
to remain decentralized and in the control of the departments, the commission was authorized to supervise the conduct of examinations and make investigations to determine

the degree of departmental enforcement of its rules. Of tremendous significance was the authority given to the president to extend merit system coverage to federal employees by executive order. However, the authority to extend also carries with it the authority to retract. Theoretically the president could reintroduce spoils into those large portions of the federal service not specifically protected by other legislation, at any time he wishes. Both Presidents McKinley and Eisenhower had occasion to remove positions from merit coverage by executive order. In both cases this resulted when a new party assumed power only to find that, in their opinion, a disproportionate number of positions had been "blanketed in" by the previous administration.

The Pendleton Act was hardly a total victory for the reformers. It only covered just over 10 percent of the federal service.[62] Actually the reformers were not at all anxious for near universal merit system coverage. They recognized the problems of creating the appropriate administrative machinery and were concerned that the reform program would be overburdened and subject to failure if complete reform were attempted all at once.[63] Over the years, federal employees were brought more and more under the jurisdiction of the Civil Service Commission or of other federal merit systems, such as those of the Foreign Service, Tennessee Valley Authority, and so forth. When the Republicans gained control of the presidency in 1969, only about 6,500 of approximately 3 million federal positions were specifically designated as patronage opportunities.[64] But remember, this is largely a self-imposed limitation.[65]

American presidents during the reform period typically entered office taking full advantage of their patronage prerogatives and left office with extensions of the merit system to their credit. This was the case with every president from Arthur to Wilson. Merit system coverage went from 10 percent in 1884 to over 70 percent by the end of World War I.[66] Generally, lame duck presidents being succeeded by someone of a different party would "blanket in" large numbers of employees in order to reduce the amount of patronage available to the opposition party. One of the ironies of civil service reform brought about by such "blanketing in" is that such initial reforms have a tendency to benefit those who may be the least meritorious. Whenever civil service rules are extended by executive or legislative fiat, the incumbents are usually given civil service protection without having to undergo formal examinations or have an overwhelming "edge" if such examina-

tions are administered. Such procedures made it easier
for retiring American presidents during the reform period
to extend the classified service to cover their party
friends. "When, however, the opposite party comes to power
and finds its opponents securely lodged in offices which
but just now were patronage and from which its own members
may have been but recently expelled, a severe strain is
put upon the belief in the morality of civil service reform;
it seems like saying that to the vanquished belong the
spoils."[67] A new twist on this old gambit was evolved when
the newly elected Democratic governor of Pennsylvania, Milton Shapp, desired to dismiss the Republic incumbents of
long-standing patronage positions. Many of the incumbents
in certain departments, anxious to retain their jobs,
quickly formed themselves into a union. When the governor
sought to dismiss them, they successfully obtained a court
injunction to retain their jobs and prevent the governor
from "busting" their union.

Presidents undoubtedly had mixed motives concerning
their last-minute extensions of the merit system. While
they sincerely wished to deny the patronage prerogatives
that they enjoyed to their successors, many had become
truly disillusioned by their experiences with spoils and
possibly repentant of their excesses. As it has not been
in the character of American presidents to be repentant,
however great may be their sins or their surface religiosi-
ty, one must assume a degree of disillusionment. The definitive statement on the disillusioning aspects of political patronage is credited to President William Howard Taft,
who was moved to conclude that whenever he made a patronage
appointment, he created "nine enemies and one ingrate."[68]
Actually this quip is generally attributed to all sophisticated dispensers of patronage from Thomas Jefferson to
Louis XIV.[69] The American presidency has produced only
two memorable patronage jokes besides many of the appointees themselves. In addition to President Taft's remark,
there is the story that Abraham Lincoln, while lying pros-
trate in the White House with an attack of smallpox, said
to his attendants: "Tell all the office-seekers to come
in at once, for now I have something I can give to all of
them."[70] Do not be too disarmed by Lincoln's humor; for
he was the most astute handler of patronage and its attendant corruption that the White House has ever seen.[71]

State governors have tended to find themselves in essentially the same patronage dilemma as presidents. Accordingly, there has been a striking similarity in conduct.
A comparison of the inaugural addresses of governors with

their subsequent farewell addresses reveals an interesting contrast in their recommendations concerning patronage. "The silence of the incoming governor is followed by statesmanlike pronouncements from the outgoing governor on behalf of a strengthened civil service."[72] An examination of the executive tendency to extend the merit system would find not so much disillusionment with past practices as a calculated effort to increase the power of the executive at the direct expense of the legislature. Because American political parties are decentralized, patronage appointments tend to be more to the advantage of local political leaders than to the executive. The conversion of patronage positions to merit system positions has the effect of taking power away from the local politicos and centralizing it in or at least having it neutralized by the executive. Consequently, presidents and governors have tended to support civil service reform while congressmen and state legislators have tended to oppose it.[73]

THE MIXED MOTIVATIONS OF THE REFORMERS

The chronology of civil service reform is easily delineated. A variety of specific events and documents have provided a convenient framework for analysis. The motivations of those who led the reform movement have remained a clouded issue lending themselves to considerable speculation. Nevertheless, an attempt to understand these motivations is essential if the structure and import of present merit system institutions are to be appreciated as the product of historical circumstances rather than divine intervention.

Historians tend to agree that the leaders of the reform movement represented a socioeconomic class that was both out of power and decidedly antagonistic to those elements of society who were in power. In simplistic terms it was the WASP patricians versus the ethnic plebeians. The social upheavals that accompanied the Civil War left in its wake what Richard Hofstadter has described as a displaced class of old gentry, professional men, and the civic leaders of an earlier time.

> In their personal careers, as in their community
> activities, they found themselves checked, ham-
> pered, and overridden by the agents of the new
> corporations, the corrupters of legislatures,
> the buyers of franchises, the allies of the po-

litical bosses. In this uneven struggle they
found themselves limited by their own scruples,
their regard for reputation, their social standing itself. To be sure, the America they knew
did not lack opportunities, but it did seem to
lack opportunities of the highest sort for men
of the highest standards. In a strictly economic
sense these men were not growing poorer as a
class, but their wealth and power were being
dwarfed by comparison with the new eminences of
wealth and power. They were less important, and
they knew it.[74]

   This displacement, this alienation, did much to establish the "ins" versus the "outs" pattern of the politics
of reform. Because the reformers blamed the professional
politicians for their own political impotence, they struck
at the source of his strength--the spoils system. "As a
weapon they used civil service reform, which would convert
the public service from partisanship to political neutrality."[75] President Grant inadvertently accelerated the demand for reform when, upon obtaining office, he not only
excluded from patronage appointments the old gentry but
also denied office to the editors of influential newspapers
and journals. This was in contrast to Lincoln's policy of
courting the press by bestowing lavish patronage upon them.
As a result the press of both parties started speaking out
more strongly than ever before in favor of reform.[76] "By
shutting the door to public service on the 'respectable and
cultured' members of society, Grant unwittingly converted
many of them to civil service reform."[77]
   Certainly the huddled polyglot masses of the country's
growing urban centers had little concern for reforming the
public service at any level of government. A sincere concern for honesty in public service has always been a luxury
reserved for the middle and upper classes. The masses
only care deeply about the integrity of public office if
it proves to have some measurable and immediate effect on
their lives. "If a choice is necessary, the populace of
an American city will choose kindness over honesty, as the
nation's enduring Tammanys attest."[78]
   While the reform impetus might strike some as being a
radical departure, its origins were essentially conserva-
tive. "Its leaders were not interested in revolutionizing
anything or even in recognizing the fundamental alteration
industrialism had made in American society."[79] The reformers "wished to return to the attitudes of the good old days

27

before Jacksonian democracy and the industrial revolution --days when men with their background, status, and education were the unquestioned leaders of society."[80] In the mind of the patrician reformer, "the ideal government tended to be one by men like himself."[81] Such men, being endowed by nature with a special grace, "would treat all problems with no urge for self-aggrandizement and would mete out to each group a disinterested justice."[82] Actually, most of the occupants of this class took a more realistic view. As so many of them enjoyed the conveniences that the spoils system brought to their business lives, they reconciled their oft-preached respect for law and order by more typically taking the view that corruption should not be "too strongly condemned, nor spoils politics too vigorously assailed."[83] This attitude and the circumstances that engendered it had a limiting effect upon the zeal of the reforming class. According to the Democratic candidate for president in 1868, Governor Horatio Seymour of New York, "our people want men in office who will not steal, but who will not interfere with those who do."[84] Some statements are timeless.[85] No less an advocate of civil service reform than Theodore Roosevelt himself was to remark that the movement was decidedly one "from above downwards."[86]

While there is no way of ascertaining for sure what particular factors engendered a reform impetus within any given individual, there is no doubt that the reform proposals themselves tended to benefit one segment of society over another. While the reformers first achieved success on the national level, the class basis of the reform impetus was essentially an urban phenomenon "strongly tainted with nativism"[87]--the WASP suburbanites, being dismayed at what the ethnic hordes were doing to "their" city, called for reform.[88] The public service has always been used by the ascending groups in American society as a vehicle for social advancement. Inevitably accompanying such changes has been a large measure of friction, distrust, and hostility. The continuity of this process is unbroken to this day. In this regard there is no significant difference between the successors of Jackson deposing the aristocratically tinged civil service to replace them with loyalists of common origin and today's displacement of white ethnic municipal officials with black stalwarts. What is happening with black groups in American cities today is the same process of assimilation and socialization, the "same 'mobility cycle' . . . which was undergone by the Irish after the Civil War, and after them the Jews and

Italians. It is a process full of corruption and full of vitality."[89] Each of these groups had a similar problem during the time that they dominated local public office. The groups that were displaced were quite vocal in indicating that the insurgents were grossly corrupt and using public office largely for their private gain and for the advantage of their peers. While such utterances are typically attributed to such factors as racism and religious prejudice, the foundation upon which these remarks are made--the venality of public office--is essentially sound. There is no doubt that each succeeding power group used public office to their private advantage. This continues today. The intent of the Jacksonian philosophy, that "success through politics . . . must become a legitimate aspiration of the many,"[90] has thus been achieved. As each succeeding social group took advantage of whatever the local political process could offer, they advanced themselves socially, sent their children to college, and moved to the suburbs leaving the machine and its style of politics to the next cycle of immigrants.[91] Now both physically and generationally removed from the political atmosphere from which they benefited, they feel comfortable in viewing the present inhabitants of the buildings in which they were born as socially and morally inferior. Safely middle class they can now afford to be reformers--especially now that reform is at somebody else's expense. The cycle is complete; they now feel as strongly about "those" people in the city as an earlier group felt about their grandfathers. The explanation for the intensity of these feelings, an intensity that feeds the racial tensions to the present day in our metropolitan areas, can perhaps be found by examining the aversion to politics exhibited by the newly arrived middle class.

> To regard politics as contrary to the public interest is consistent with the middle-class ideal; reformers have always taken this view. That the "new immigrants," once they have been assimilated into the middle class, should be contemptuous of politics is to be expected. There are indications, however, that their contempt for it is stronger than can be accounted for on these grounds alone. Perhaps it is in part symbolic-- a gesture meant to repudiate not the style of politics alone but also, and perhaps mainly, the inferior class and ethnic status from which it sprang.[92]

Even assuming sympathetic attitudes on the part of the now socially conscious middle class, the manifestations of these attitudes are frequently dysfunctional to the aims of the "new immigrants." The middle-class idea of doing "good" for the lower class frequently means abolishing the means by which they themselves escaped from it. While the programs of President Johnson's "war on poverty" may or may not have significantly reduced the incidence of poverty in the United States, it did provide a patronage boom for the black community. When many of these programs were found to have unaccounted-for expenditures, padded payrolls, and little effect, indignant liberals and outraged conservatives would point to black leadership and say, "You've run these programs no better than the old-style corrupt machine politicians." The general reply of some of the more outspoken black leaders was, quite simply, "Why not? It was our turn!" And so it was. In achieving the Jacksonian intent, all segments of American society have been able to better themselves through politics; and having done so, move on to disdain it. This author would not have been able to begin college immediately following high school had it not been for a politically obtained state scholarship. Had such rewards been given fairly and upon merit, there is no doubt that this author would have been excluded immediately upon the examination of his high school record. Such patronage in the form of a scholarship eventually led to middle-class respectability, a home in the suburbs, and the leisure to write books on public personnel administration. The essence of this brief biography has occurred millions of times over. To deny the current inhabitants of the central city the means by which the white ethnic groups advanced themselves is as ethically dubious as many of the patronage practices that one might wish to see abolished. To ask the lower class to play middle-class politics is to change the rules of the game just when it is their turn to play.[93] The import of this discussion is not to speak out in favor of corruption, but merely to observe some of its beneficial manifestations. The moral issues involved remain unresolved.

As the American economy expanded during the last half of the 19th century, the orientation of the business community became less and less focused on parochial interests bounded by the neighborhood and more and more oriented toward urban, regional, national, and international markets. Economic determinists could well argue that the death knell of the spoils system was sounded when the ineptness of government began to hamper the expansion of business. It is

30

noteworthy in this respect that the federal government made some efforts to institute merit system concepts in both the New York Post Office and the New York Custom House several years before the passage of the Pendleton Act. Such reform measures, limited as they were, were a direct result of pressure from a business community that had grown increasingly intolerant of ineptness in the postal service[94] and extortion on the waterfront.[95]

With the ever-present impetus of achieving maximum public services for minimum tax dollars, the businessman was quite comfortable in supporting civil service reform. Support for reform was just one of a variety of strategies employed by the business interests to have power pass from the politicos to themselves. The political parties of the time were almost totally dependent for a financial base upon assessments made on the wages of their members in public office. The party faithful had long been expected to kick back a percentage of their salary in order to retain their positions. A good portion of the Pendleton Act is devoted to forbidding this and other related methods of extortion. With the decline of patronage, the parties had to seek out new funding sources. The business interests then as now were more than quite willing to assume this new financial burden and its concomitant influence. A similar gambit used at the municipal level was to change the form of legislative representation to one elected on a city-wide basis. "Securing election in an at-large system usually required access to the newspapers, substantial campaign funds, and a reputation as one of the city's leading citizens. Prominent business or professional men could easily meet these requirements, while workers and small shopkeepers could not."[96] The business interests had an even greater advantage if there was a nonpartisan ballot. This feature of most commission-manager plans, "widely heralded as a great advance in democracy, also tended to operate against minority groups."[97] The "independent" civil service commission viewed in this perspective was just another effort to take a measure of power away from the dominant political forces represented by the ethnic machine and transfer it to those who were, in their own opinion, more deserving of it. On the national level the basic reform tactic involved centralizing civil service authority in the president while, conversely, on the local level the tactic was to deprive, as much as possible, the executive of authority over the civil service.

Governmental reform was one of the great moral issues of the reform era. With the abolition of slavery, the immorality of our governing institutions became the great moral issue that was to inspire countless journalists and opposition politicians. Moral actions based upon the Judeo-Christian heritage of Western culture are not so common in everyday life that they can be accepted at face value by those driven by either their own innate cynicism or the tenets of social science to find "other" motives. There are always a few individuals, usually out of step with their times, calling upon the public or the government to do something simply because it is the "right" thing to do. It is difficult if not impossible to separate the moralistic from the political motivations of people. One can never truly know where moral indignation over patronage abuses ended and a not disinterested concern for denying a power base to the incumbents began. It is a question that lends itself to extensive and pointless philosophic debate. There was certainly moral indignation enough to go around.[98] It is no exaggeration to say that the government service "had become permeated with a class of men who were tempted to anticipate future removal by present corruption."[99] There is no doubt that having the moral issues on their side gave the reformers a decided advantage, but it was not decisive. It is as impossible to assign weights to the myriad factors that led to the reformers' successes as it is to ascertain what influences motivated them as individuals. Individual motives were doubtelessly as mixed and subtle as the factors of success.

THE GROWTH OF THE "INDEPENDENT" CIVIL SERVICE COMMISSION

Influenced by the example of the 1883 Pendleton Act, state and local jurisdictions began to institute civil service commissions. But this was a very slow process. While New York adopted a merit system that same year and Massachusetts did so during the following year, it was more than 20 years before another state did so in 1905. By 1935 only 12 states had formally instituted merit systems.[100] These early efforts were not all successes. Connecticut had its first civil service law repealed, while Kansas kept the statute as law but "made it innocuous by refusing to vote appropriations."[101] Nor were these laws necessarily effective even when kept on the books. For example, New York State, which since 1883 had the most stringent prohibitions against political assessments on the salaries of public employees, had widespread "voluntary" contributions to the party "paid and collected without any effort toward concealment"[102] at least through the 1930s. Today all but nine of the states lack general merit system coverage for their employees.[103]

Only 65 cities had created civil service commissions by 1900. By 1930 that number had risen to 250.[104] Today less than 12 percent of cities with populations exceeding 50,000 do not have merit systems. The percentage lacking merit system coverage is almost double that for all cities in the 25,000 to 50,000 population range.[105]

Only six of the more than 3,000 counties had adopted merit systems by 1933.[106] Today only about 5 percent have instituted general merit systems.[107]

The reader should be aware that all statistics concerning merit system coverage are inherently deceptive. While such figures may be numerically accurate, they merely indicate that merit systems are "on the books," not that they exist in practice. Judging a merit system by its legal mandates is much like counting the virgins at a high school graduation. In both cases the kind of research necessary to ascertain the truth is exceedingly difficult methodologically and likely to be embarrassing to the subjects under scrutiny. The surveys of merit system coverage that are annually undertaken by a variety of good government groups are typically administered by mailed questionnaire. These statistics are by no means ascertained by empirical investigation. Consequently, while the arithmetic of these surveys may be impeccable, the resulting summaries frequently belie the true extent of merit system coverage.[108] Remember, the city of Chicago has an excellent merit system on the books, yet it manages to retain its well-earned reputation as the large American city most famous for its patronage abuses.

Subnational jurisdictions followed the federal merit system example in many respects: bipartisan civil service commissions became common, examining methods and related administrative detail were frequently similar, and prohibitions concerning assessments and other varieties of political interference were legally binding many years before a general pattern of compliance appeared. In some areas, such as position classifications programs and retirement provisions, a variety of local jurisdictions were many years ahead of the federal service. However, at the local level the pattern of reform that evolved contained a crucial difference--the civil service commission was made administratively and presumably politically independent of the jurisdiction's chief executive officer. The commission format was mandated by political, not administrative, considerations. Then as now the illogic of divorcing the control of personnel from programmatic authority was recognized. Nevertheless, the more immediate goal of defeating the influences of spoils was paramount. With this in mind, the rationale for the commission device was quite reasonable. Not only would it be independent from the party-controlled government, but its three- or five-part membership would be in a better position to resist political pressures than could any single administrator.[109] Appellate functions, especially, are better undertaken by a tribunal than by a solitary judge. Not insignificantly, a commission provides a political safety valve by making room for "special interest representation, such as racial, religious, or employee groups."[110]

It was not very long before the rationale for the independent commission was seriously challenged. As the city manager movement developed early in this century, managers --nonpartisan reform-type managers at that--found themselves burdened with the same kinds of restrictions upon their authority over personnel that had been designed to thwart the spoilsmen. These managers thus asserted that "the original reason for establishing an independent personnel agency, namely, lack of confidence in the appointing authority, does not exist with regard to them."[111] They felt, quite reasonably, that the personnel function should be integrated with the other administrative functions under the executive. The convincing nature of this argument is evidenced by the fact that almost a quarter of the jurisdictions in the United States that report having merit systems presently operate without a civil service commission.[112]

While this line of reasoning made considerable headway where the city manager concept was firmly entrenched, it had little applicability for most of the larger cities where merit system provisions implemented only a few years earlier had degenerated into a sham. Numerous accounts of the period indicate that many merit systems were such in name only.[113] This was achieved by the dual process of appointing persons unsympathetic to merit system ideals as civil service commissioners and by restricting the work of the commission by denying adequate appropriations. "The last stand of the spoilsman is usually an effort to starve into helpless inactivity the official body by which the principles of the merit system are to be enforced."[114] In response to such "starve 'em out" tactics, many jurisdictions later enacted ordinances providing that a fixed

percentage of each year's budget would be for the administration of the merit system.[115]

The advent of the civil service commission as a political device was not synonymous with the development of personnel administration as such. The commission impetus was
decidedly negative and heavily moralistic. Its goals were
to smite out "evil" as personified by the spoils system.
Viewed historically and dispassionately, one could argue
that considerable good in the guise of executive discretion also got washed away with the evil. Frederick C.
Mosher sees two lasting efforts from the widespread implementation of civil service commissions. They not only
"perpetuated the association of public personnel and its
administration with morality," but they also "divorced personnel administration from general management--from the
executives responsible for carrying on the programs and
activities of governments."[116] Mosher alludes to the central paradox of public personnel administration that William Seal Carpenter explicitly states. While the merit
system did much to improve the caliber of public employees,
it "seldom has helped the chief executive to gain control
of the administration he is by law directed to perform."[117]
While civil service reform did much to curtail the disabling effects of spoils, it did not at the same time
"create adequate standards of personnel administration."[118]
Unlike its private sector counterpart, the personnel function in government has two frequently conflicting roles.
Of necessity it must attend both to service and to control.
Is it possible to be both an integral member of the management team and be the organization's policeman at the same
time? Yet this is the role that a personnel officer in
the public sector is usually called upon to play. This
uncomfortable condition has frequently been discussed.
Norman J. Powell eloquently summarizes the problem: "To
enforce civil service rules and law involves connotations,
practices, and an orientation different from those imbedded
in being servitor to the executive."[119] In its various
manifestations, this is the central dilemma of public personnel administration today.

NOTES

1. William E. Mosher and J. Donald Kingsley, Public
Personnel Administration (New York: Harper & Bros., 1936),
p. xiii. This is the first edition of what has become O.
Glenn Stahl's text, now in its sixth edition.

2. E. A. Kracke, Jr., "Bureaucratic Recruitment and Advancement in Imperial China," in Michael T. Dalby and Michael S. Werthman, eds., Bureaucracy in Historical Perspective (Glenview, Ill.: Scott, Foresman and Co., 1971), pp. 34-39. For a broader perspective, see Claude S. George, Jr., The History of Management Thought, 2d ed. (Englewood Cliffs, N.J.: Prentice-Hall, 1972), pp. 4-27; E. N. Gladden, A History of Public Administration (London: Frank Cass, 1972), vol. 2.

3. An excellent history of this development is Hans Rosenberg, Bureaucracy, Aristocracy and Autocracy: The Prussian Experience 1660-1815 (Cambridge, Mass.: Harvard University Press, 1958).

4. Descriptions of Weber's model of bureaucracy are found in most textbooks dealing with organizational phenomena. For the original source, in translation, of course, see H. H. Gerth and C. Wright Mills, From Max Weber: Essays in Sociology (New York: Oxford University Press, 1946).

5. For a discussion of Weber's significance, see Howard E. McCurdy, Public Administration: A Bibliography (Washington, D.C.: College of Public Affairs, American University, 1972), pp. 9 ff.

6. Leonard D. White, The Jeffersonians (New York: Macmillan, 1951), p. 351.

7. Ibid., p. 352-54.

8. For an analysis of the elitist nature of the federal service through Jackson's time, see Sidney H. Aronson, Status and Kinship in the Higher Civil Service (Cambridge, Mass.: Harvard University Press, 1964). Also see the administrative histories of Leonard D. White, The Federalists, The Jeffersonians, The Jacksonians (New York: Macmillan, 1948; 1951; 1954).

9. For an analysis of Jackson's removals see Erik M. Eriksson, "The Federal Civil Service Under President Jackson," Mississippi Valley Historical Review 13 (March 1927): 517-40. Eriksson's conclusions are confirmed by both Aronson, Status and Kinship in the Higher Civil Service, and White, The Jacksonians.

10. Samuel Eliot Morison, The Oxford History of the American People (New York: Oxford University Press, 1965), p. 426.

11. Charles Cooke, Biography of an Ideal: The Diamond Anniversary History of the Federal Civil Service (Washington, D.C.: U.S. Government Printing Office, 1959), p. 20. The intensity of the Senate's quarrels with Jackson over his appointments is illustrated by this 1832 debate where

the Senate refused "to confirm the appointment of Martin Van Buren, earlier approved as Secretary of State, as ambassador to Great Britain, after Van Buren had already arrived in Europe." Paul P. Van Riper, History of the United States Civil Service (Evanston, Ill.: Row, Peterson & Co., 1958), p. 38.

12. White, The Jacksonians, p. 374. Marcy actually had his program approved by the Congress, but the authorizing legislation was repealed before anyone could be appointed.

13. "Between 1812 and 1821 six western states entered the Union with constitutions providing for universal white manhood suffrage or a close approximation, and between 1810 and 1821 four of the older states substantially dropped property qualifications for voters. As poor farmers and workers gained the ballot, there developed a type of politician that had existed only in embryo in the Jeffersonian period--the technician of mass leadership, the caterer to mass sentiment; it was a coterie of such men in all parts of the country that converged upon the prominent figure of Jackson between 1815 and 1824." Richard Hofstadter, The American Political Tradition (New York: Vintage Books, 1948), p. 50.

14. Van Riper, History of the United States Civil Service, p. 36.

15. Normal Mailer, Miami and the Siege of Chicago (New York: Signet, 1968), pp. 105 ff. Mailer credits political columnist Murray Kempton with aiding him with this insight.

16. Van Riper, History of the United States Civil Service, p. 36.

17. Ibid., p. 37.

18. Arthur M. Schlesinger, Jr., The Age of Jackson (Boston: Little, Brown and Co., 1945), p. 46.

19. Ibid.

20. Aronson, Status and Kinship in the Higher Civil Service, p. 195.

21. Van Riper, History of the United States Civil Service, p. 37.

22. For example, see Howard Lee McBain, DeWitt Clinton and the Origin of the Spoils System in New York (New York: AMS Press, Inc., 1967).

23. Actually, Jackson was a conspicuous symbol for a great many things. See John William Ward, Andrew Jackson: Symbol for an Age (New York: Oxford University Press, 1962).

24. Van Riper, History of the United States Civil Service, pp. 35-36.

25. White, The Jacksonians, p. 312.

26. Ibid., p. 314.

27. David Donald, Lincoln Reconsidered (New York: Knopf, 1959), pp. 71-81.

28. Donald R. Harvey, The Civil Service Commission (New York: Praeger, 1970), p. 5.

29. Van Riper, History of the United States Civil Service, p. 43.

30. Ibid., p. 44.

31. White, The Jacksonians, p. 362.

32. White, The Jeffersonians, pp. 363-65.

33. Ibid., pp. 365-66.

34. Ibid., pp. 370-71. This legislation remained in effect until it was superceded by the Pendleton Act of 1883.

35. For a thoroughly detailed account of Jenckes' reform proposals and his motivations, see Ari Hoogenboom, Outlawing the Spoils: A History of the Civil Service Reform Movement: 1865-1883 (Urbana: University of Illinois Press, 1961), pp. 14-63. An earlier reform bill was introduced by Senator Charles Sumner, Republican of Massachusetts, in 1864, but it received little attention.

36. Carl Russell Fish, The Civil Service and the Patronage (New York: Russell & Russell, 1904, 1963), p. 212.

37. Hoogenboom, Outlawing the Spoils, p. 60.

38. Ibid., p. 32.

39. White, The Republican Era, p. 281.

40. Ibid., p. 286.

41. Ibid., p. 282. Also supporting this view is Van Riper, History of the United States Civil Service, p. 68.

42. For a brief account of the role that the press played in the reform effort, see Charles J. Nelson, "The Press and Civil Service Reform," Civil Service Journal 13 (April-June 1973): 1-3.

43. Sixteen U.S.C. § 514 (1871); Rev. Stats. § 1753, as cited in White, The Republican Era, pp. 281-82; and Van Riper, History of the United States Civil Service, p. 68.

44. Frank Mann Stewart, The National Civil Service Reform League: History, Activities, Problems (Austin: University of Texas, 1929), p. 21.

45. Curtis was later to become the first president of the National Civil Service Reform League upon its creation in 1881.

46. After the commission was abolished, "appointments reverted to the pass examination system established by the Act of 1853." White, The Republican Era, p. 284.

47. Lionel V. Murphy, "The First Federal Civil Service Commission: 1871-1875," Public Personnel Review 3 (October 1942): 323.

48. The "rule of three" was devised not necessarily to give greater discretion to appointing authorities, but in response to an opinion by the attorney general that the certification of a single individual "would impose an unconstitutional limitation on the appointing power." Van Riper, History of the United States Civil Service, p. 107.

49. The Pendleton bill as originally drafted contained this provision, but it was discarded during the Senate debate. Van Riper, History of the United States Civil Service, p. 100.

50. White, The Republican Era, p. 284.

51. Jean J. Couturier, "The Model Public Personnel Administration Law: Two Views--Pro," Public Personnel Review 32 (October 1971): 209.

52. Stewart, The National Civil Service Reform League, p. 28.

53. Ibid., pp. 24-25.

54. Matthew Josephson, The Politicos: 1865-1896 (New York: Harcourt, Brace & Company, 1938), p. 315.

55. Ibid., p. 319. Although insanity was raised as a defense at his trial, Guiteau was executed anyway during the following year.

56. Hoogenboom, Outlawing the Spoils, p. 212.

57. James Bryce, The American Commonwealth, new ed. (New York: Macmillan, 1971), vol. 2, p. 26. The insincerity of the major parties toward civil service reform is discussed by E. E. Schattschneider, who upon noting that from 1872 to 1900 the platforms of each national party was pledged to reform, observed: "Having thus discovered the steady purpose of the parties to abolish the spoils system throughout the fourth quarter of the nineteenth century, the student will be puzzled to find that a generation later . . . the parties are still firmly resolved to abolish this ancient evil." Party Government (New York: Farrar and Rinehart, 1942), p. 139.

58. Darrell Hevenor Smith, The United States Civil Service Commission: Its History, Activities and Organization (Baltimore: The Johns Hopkins Press, 1928), p. 12. Also discussed by Van Riper, History of the United States Civil Service, p. 65.

59. Dorman B. Eaton, <u>Civil Service in Great Britain</u> (New York: Harper & Bros., 1880). For a broader perspective of the British Civil Service, see E. N. Gladden, <u>Civil Services of the United Kingdom</u> (New York: Augustus M. Kelley, 1967).

60. The exam was for junior personnel examiner positions at the commission itself. John M. Pfiffner, <u>Public Administration</u> (New York: Ronald Press, 1935), p. 173.

61. A 1935 survey found that "no provision has been made for drawing college men into executive work in state and municipal governments, and as the departments are at present organized there is no place to use college men effectively." George A. Graham, "Personnel Practices in Business and Governmental Organizations," in Carl J. Friedrich et al., <u>Problems of the American Public Service</u> (New York: McGraw Hill, 1935), p. 430. John M. Pfiffner wrote that "the men making the civil service laws have frequently been of the 'self-made' variety, distrusting attempts to establish scholarship standards." <u>Public Administration</u>, pp. 170-71.

62. Of the 132,800 positions then in the federal service, 13,900 were placed in the competitive civil service system. Cooke, <u>Biography of an Ideal</u>, p. 57.

63. Van Riper cites the Senate testimony of Dorman B. Easton to this effect, <u>History of the United States Civil Service</u>, p. 105. Also discussed in Stewart, <u>The National Civil Service Reform League</u>.

64. <u>Congressional Quarterly</u>, January 3, 1969, p. 15.

65. For an itemized list of federal patronage in 1973, see Committee on Post Office and Civil Service, U.S. Senate, 93rd Cong., 1st Sess., <u>United States Government Policy and Supporting Positions</u> (Washington, D.C.: U.S. Government Printing Office, 1973).

66. A blow-by-blow description of this gradual extension is provided by Stewart, <u>The National Civil Service Reform League</u>, pp. 48-70.

67. Fish, <u>The Civil Service and the Patronage</u>, p. 223.

68. Louis W. Koenig, <u>The Chief Executive</u>, rev. ed. (New York: Harcourt, Brace & World, 1968), p. 97.

69. This quip seems more apocryphal than assignable. Norman J. Powell credits it to Louis XIV. <u>Personnel Administration in Government</u> (Englewood Cliffs, N.J.: Prentice-Hall, 1956), p. 88. Leonard D. White credits the phrase to Thomas Jefferson, who, because he said it in French, may have been quoting Louis XIV. <u>The Jeffersonians</u>, p. 349.

70. Cooke, Biography of an Ideal, p. 34.

71. For discussions of how Lincoln held the Union together with patronage, see Donald, Lincoln Reconsidered,
pp. 71-81; Harry J. Carman and Reinhard H. Luthin, Lincoln
and the Patronage (New York: Columbia University Press,
1943).

72. Daniel R. Grant and H. C. Nixon, State and Local
Government in America, 2d ed. (Boston: Allyn and Bacon,
1968), p. 348.

73. E. E. Schattschneider, Party Government, pp. 137-
40.

74. Richard Hofstadter, The Age of Reform (New York:
Vintage Books, 1955), p. 137.

75. Hoogenboom, Outlawing the Spoils, p. ix.

76. Ibid., pp. 63-64.

77. Ibid., p. 70.

78. Hofstadter, The American Political Tradition, p.
177.

79. Hoogenboom, Outlawing the Spoils, p. 197.

80. Ibid.

81. Eric F. Goldman, Rendezvous with Destiny: A History of Modern American Reform (New York: Knopf, 1965),
pp. 18-19.

82. Ibid., p. 19.

83. C. E. Merriam, American Political Ideas (New York:
Macmillan, 1920), p. 28, as cited in Josephson, The Politicos, p. 149.

84. Seymour's comment upon the reform movement was
made in a letter to Samuel Tilden. Josephson, The Politicos, p. 153.

85. Anyone doubting the persistent veracity of Seymour's statement is invited to read Brian D. Boyer, Cities
Destroyed for Cash: The FHA Scandal at HUD (Chicago: Follett Publishing Co., 1973).

86. Goldman, Rendezvous with Destiny, p. 19.

87. Hofstadter, The Age of Reform, p. 178.

88. For an analysis of this phenomenon, see Richard
C. Wade, "The Periphery Versus the Center," in Bruce M.
Stave, ed., Urban Bosses, Machines, and Progressive Re-
formers (Lexington, Mass.: D. C. Heath, 1972), pp. 75-80.
For an analysis of the long-standing antipathy toward the
city by the intellectual classes in America, see Morton
and Lucia White, The Intellectual Versus the City: From
Thomas Jefferson to Frank Lloyd Wright (Cambridge, Mass.:
Harvard University Press, 1962).

89. Eric L. McKitrik, "The Study of Corruption," in
James F. Richardson, ed., The American City: Historical

Studies (Waltham, Mass.: Xerox College Publishing, 1972),
pp. 187-88. Originally appeared in Political Science Quarterly 72 (December 1957): 502-514.

90. Hofstadter, The American Political Tradition, p.
51.

91. The Nixon administration gave tacit recognition
to this phenomena when Daniel Moynihan, as the president's
domestic adviser, advocated a policy of "benign neglect"
for our urban areas.

92. Edward C. Banfield and James Q. Wilson, City Politics (New York: Vintage Books, 1963), p. 331.

93. "In politics as in everything else it makes a
great difference whose game we play. The rules of the
game determine the requirements for success." E. E.
Schattschneider, The Semi-Sovereign People: A Realist's
View of Democracy in America (New York: Holt, Rinehart
and Winston, 1960), p. 48.

94. Hoogenboom, Outlawing the Spoils, p. 14.

95. Josephson, The Politicos, p. 241; White, The Republican Era, pp. 118-26.

96. James Weinstein, "The Small Businessman as Big
Businessman: The City Commissioner and Management Move-
ments," in James F. Richardson, ed., The American City:
Historical Studies (Waltham, Mass.: Xerox College Publishing, 1972), p. 218. Also see James Weinstein, The Corporate Ideal in the Liberal State in 1900-1818 (Boston: Beacon Press, 1968).

97. Richardson, The American City, p. 227. Substantial empirical evidence suggests that with the absence of
parties, political campaigns tend to turn on trivial personal attributes, influence shifts to nonparty groups,
there is less campaigning, and protest voting is frustrated.
Fred I. Greenstein, The American Party System and the American People (Englewood Cliffs, N.J.: Prentice-Hall, 1963),
pp. 58-60.

98. For a strong dose of modern-day indignation, see
Martin and Susan Tolchin, To the Victor: Political Pa-
tronage from the Clubhouse to the White House (New York:
Random House, 1971).

99. Morison, The Oxford History of the American People, p. 736.

100. The 12 states with merit systems before 1935 were
New York (1883), Massachusetts (1884), Wisconsin (1905),
Illinois (1905), Colorado (1970), New Jersey (1908), Ohio
(1912), California (1913), Connecticut (1913), Kansas
(1916), Maryland (1920), Michigan (1935). Mosher and
Kingsley, Public Personnel Administration, p. 29.

101. Ibid.

102. Ibid., p. 23.

103. These are Mississippi, Missouri, Montana, Nebraska, North Dakota, South Carolina, Tennessee, Texas, West Virginia. Book of the States: 1972-1973 (Lexington, Ky.: Council of State Governments, 1972), pp. 176-79.

104. Leonard D. White, Trends in Public Administration (New York: McGraw-Hill, 1933), p. 246. White notes that in addition about 400 city manager cities "have almost without exception a real merit system, although usually no civil service commission." The statistics of merit system expansion during this period seem to conflict because of quibbles over what constitutes a merit system. For slightly higher figures, see International City Manager's Association, Municipal Personnel Administration, 6th ed. (Chicago: ICMA, 1960), p. 15.

105. The Municipal Year Book (Washington, D.C.: International City Management Association, issued annually). See also Jacob J. Rutstein, "Survey of Current Personnel Systems in State and Local Governments," Good Government 87 (Spring 1971): 1-28.

106. Mosher and Kinglsey, Public Personnel Administration, p. 30.

107. O. Glenn Stahl, Public Personnel Administration, 5th ed. (New York: Harper & Row, 1962), p. 46. This figure excludes public school personnel.

108. The deceptive nature of merit system statistics has not gone completely unnoticed by others. For example, Leo Kramer has written that "cities without civil service tend to report less diligently than those with civil service. And some systems that reported complete coverage show, on closer inspection, exclusions by law or practice. The situation in the country service is more difficult to estimate and probably represents the lowest percentage of civil service coverage, being, in some areas, the last outpost of the spoils system. While figures are more easily available for the state services, they must be accepted as only approximations that give an impression of exaggerated coverage." Labor's Paradox: The American Federation of State, County, and Municipal Employees AFL-CIO (New York: Wiley, 1962), pp. 29-30.

109. Lewis Meriam, Public Personnel Problems: From the Standpoint of the Operating Officer (Washington, D.C.: Brookings Institution, 1938), pp. 350-51.

110. Leonard D. White, Introduction to the Study of Public Administration, 4th ed. (New York: Macmillan, 1955), p. 319. As ethnic groups sought power in America,

they used as a crude index of their power the sheer numbers of their group attaining visible public office. Theodore J. Lowi has shown that municipal appointments in New
York City very much reflected this process. At the Pleasure of the Mayor: Patronage and Power in New York City,
1898-1958 (New York: The Free Press, 1964), pp. 51-52.

111. White, Trends in Public Administration, p. 239.

112. Rutstein, "Survey of Current Personnel Systems
in State and Local Governments," p. 2.

113. A. Chester Hanford, Problems in Municipal Govern-
ment (Chicago: A. W. Shaw, 1926), pp. 196-212; John M.
Pfiffner, Municipal Administration (New York: Ronald
Press, 1940), p. 130.

114. William C. Beyer, "Recent Improvements in Methods
of Recruiting the Public Service," in Edward A. Fitzpatrick,
ed., Experts in City Government (New York: D. Appleton,
1919), p. 201.

115. For example, The Philadelphia Home Rule Charter,
as adopted by the electors on April 17, 1951.

116. Frederick C. Mosher, Democracy and the Public Service (New York: Oxford University Press, 1968), p. 70.

117. William Seal Carpenter, The Unfinished Business of
Civil Service Reform (Princeton, N.J.: Princeton University Press, 1952), p. 28.

118. Ibid.

119. Powell, Personnel Administration in Government,
p. 164. For a similar statement, see Meriam, Public Personnel Problems, p. 343. Such administrative role conflicts
are not limited to public personnel programs. Speaking
generally, Douglas McGregor observes that "the necessity
for role flexibility sometimes places the manager in an
impossible situation. This happens when he is forced to
occupy incompatible roles in a relationship with another
individual or a group. Performance appraisal programs,
for example, often require the superior to occupy simul-
taneously the role of judge and the role of counselor to
a subordinate. Members of staff departments are frequently
required to be specialists offering professional service
and advice, and in addition, policemen administering managerial controls." The Human Side of Enterprise (New York:
McGraw-Hill, 1960), p. 29-30.

3

**A FUNNY THING
HAPPENED ON THE WAY
TO CIVIL SERVICE
REFORM—MERIT
GOT LOST**

There has long been considerable agreement among those intimately familiar with public personnel operations that somewhere along the road of civil service reform, merit got lost. Practitioners and academics from Woodrow Wilson, who was both, to the present have been so concerned with the problem of achieving politically neutral competence that they have tended to lose sight of the related problem of politically neutral incompetence. The reform movement as a matter of strategy held that politics should be removed from the business of government. The movement's most eloquent and erudite spokesman, Woodrow Wilson, maintained in his famous 1887 article, "The Study of Administration," that "administration lies outside the proper sphere of politics. Administrative questions are not political questions. Although politics sets the tasks for administration, it should not be suffered to manipulate its offices."[1] While a variety of writers have expanded upon the themes established by Wilson, Herbert Kaufman has best articulated the desire of the reformers by labeling it the "quest for neutral competence."[2] The quest, begun almost a century ago, has never waned.[3] But while the quest has noble origins and commendable intent, it has brought in its wake the pollutant of mediocrity. This observation, unfortunately, is neither current nor novel. It has long been noted that "the battle against the spoilsman has made civil service reformers more intent on competence before appointments than upon performance after appointments."[4]

As the reform movement made inroads—as competence became neutral—its obvious flaw came to the surface. Writing in 1904, Carl Russell Fish observed that

> an entirely different class of men is attracted
> into the service. Under the old lack of system,
> any position might lead anywhere, and that
> quickly; removal was constantly impending; gov-
> ernment service was speculative, and because of
> the opportunities it afforded attracted clever,
> sometimes brilliant, men. Now it offers, in the
> main, the advantage of steady, light employment
> at a moderate remuneration and attracts the steady-
> going and unimaginative.[5]

Sixty years later the Municipal Manpower Commission reaf-
firmed Fish's pessimistic view when it concluded that local
governments were "not supported by personnel systems aimed
at providing personnel of superior ability."[6] The commission lamented that the major contribution to this poor
managerial posture was the severely restricted authority
of management for personnel actions.[7] As discussed earlier,
one of the lasting legacies of the reform movement, with
its emphasis upon the creation of independent civil service
commissions, was the divorcing of personnel administration
from general management. How did this unfortunate situation develop? It was certainly not the intent of the reformers that the public service should become dominated
by those seeking small jobs and great security. The impetus of the reform movement was of necessity essentially
negative--destroy the spoils system--rather than positive.
In the last century the scope of governmental operations
was of such a dimension that the managerial implications
of reform were hardly relevant. Besides, for the time,
the abolition of spoils alone was a major managerial improvement in itself because it frequently implied that the
incumbent would actually perform the duties of his position. By and large, the extent of concern for positive
personnel management was evidenced by the impetus for position classification programs that offered the radical idea
of equal pay for equal work. But classification programs
did not come into fashion until the second two decades of
this century.[8] Personnel management during the early reform period was limited to the essentials: discovering
who was on the payroll, providing equitable salaries,
and recording attendance. The reform task was so immense
that the emphasis had to be on the negative policing aspects of personnel management--that in itself was positive.

The original intent of the reformers has tended to be
forgotten or misinterpreted. A partial return to these
original precepts of civil service reform would go far

toward reconciling the artificial separation of personnel from management.

Historically the merit system was introduced to supersede the spoils system. That is to say, appointments to jobs were to be on a basis of merit and fitness, and protection against dismissal for political, racial, or religious reasons was guaranteed. Security of tenure was not intended to protect incompetence or misconduct. The appointing authority was not to be restricted in the internal operations of his department by the adoption of the merit system. Rather what he must do is to make his appointments from civil service eligible lists. What he must not do is to discriminate among his employees on political, racial, or religious grounds. It was never the purpose of the merit system to transfer to the central personnel agency the control of public employees so that the heads of operating departments lost their authority effectively to deal with them.[9]

The reformers tended to think that if the front door or entrance to the civil service was protected from political influences, then the back door or the question of removals would take care of itself. Theoretically, there would be no incentive for a politically appointed or elected executive to remove an otherwise competent employee if he could not be replaced by a political cohort. Accordingly, the Pendleton Act of 1883 and subsequent state and local legislation made no provision for removals. The reform movement leaders actually quite openly supported management's absolute prerogative of removal for all but religious or political reasons. George William Curtis, one of the founders in 1881 and later the president of the National Civil Service Reform League, was quite supportive of management's unimparied discretion. In commenting upon removal restrictions, he declared that "it is better to take the risk of occasional injustice from passion and prejudice, which no law or regulation can control, than to seal up incompetency, negligence, insubordination, insolence, and every other mischief in the service, by requiring a virtual trial at law before an unfit or incapable clerk can be removed."[10]

Viewed historically, it was the persistent abuse of management's prerogative of removal that led to its curtailment. The new federal civil service law had hardly been in effect when it developed that removals were commonly being made for partisan reasons. The Civil Service Commission reported that it was common for employees of one political faith to be dismissed "for offenses which were allowed to pass unnoticed or with a slight reprimand when committed by employees of the opposite party."[11] In addition there developed the increasingly common practice of removals upon secret charges, especially in the Post Office Department. This led the highly influential National Civil Service Reform League in 1886 to advocate that the reasons for any and all removals should be placed upon the public record.[12] However, it was not until 1897 that an executive order of President McKinley provided that removals were not to be made in the competitive service except for just cause and upon written charges. The aggrieved employee was to be entitled to a reasonable time for answering any such charges. While this was altogether a just thing to do, it opened the door to so many procedural safeguards for employees that removal power, for all practical purposes, no longer lay with management but with outside judicial or quasi-judicial agencies.

The Lloyd LaFollette Act of 1912, expanding upon an executive order of President Roosevelt, required that removals were to be made only to promote the efficiency of the service. While employees were entitled to notice, charges, and an opportunity to reply, final authority remained with department heads, and there was no appeal for a reversal to either the Civil Service Commission or the courts.[13] It was not until the 1940s that this situation changed under the dual impetus of legislative provisions for civil rights and veterans' preference. The Ramspeck Act of 1940 prohibited discrimination in federal employment because of race, color, or creed, thus providing for the first time a binding appeal beyond the department level. Because this provision of the law was poorly enforced, it had little real impact. However, the Veteran's Preference Act of 1944 established the right of veterans to appeal dismissals to the Civil Service Commission. Since more than half of the postwar federal service consisted of veterans, this changed the whole nature of removal proceedings. According to the second Hoover Commission, the impact of the Veteran's Act "was to close the 'open back door' which had always existed in the Federal civil service system."[14] For the first time department heads and their assistants had to approach dismissal action with the thought that they might have to justify such action to a neutral third party or have their actions reversed. Subsequent civil rights and related legislation has given all federal employees possible grounds with which to appeal dismissal actions to the Civil Service Commission or to the courts.[15] The removal procedures have now become so cumbersome and time consuming for a manager that marginal employees are tolerated where they once were not. It is frequently easier to seek additional staff than to remove those that are incompetent. In this regard we have come full circle. A long-recognized fault of the spoils system was the creation of otherwise unnecessary positions to compensate for the inadequacies of political appointees.[16] Public managers are still doing the same today, but now they are doing so to compensate for their merit system employees who are unproductive. While not universally true, this tendency remains disturbingly valid.

The growth of procedural inhibitions of removals at the local level has been a similar story. Because employees who had been appointed following competitive examinations tended to be removed arbitrarily, presumably for political reasons, restrictions evolved upon the appointing officer's removal power. The first kind of restriction was typically a requirement that an employee facing removal be given a written statement of the reasons for his pending dismissal. While the employee had an opportunity to reply, he had no opportunity for appeal unless the removal was for political or religious reasons. Only then would a civil service commission have the right to review and possibly reverse the decision. Generally speaking, "civil service reform in its initial stages in the United States was satisfied to leave in the hands of administrative officials complete control of the public employees after these had been selected following open competition."[17] As abuses of the new merit system became more common, greater restrictions came to be placed upon the appointing officer. In effect the power to remove an employee was taken away from the appointing authority and give to the personnel agency, usually a civil service commission. The state of Illinois pioneered with this development in 1895 by requiring that employees be removed only "for cause" and providing for a formal hearing where an employee could oppose the dismissal with a defense. The policy of using the civil service commission as an appeals board for disciplinary actions was eventually incorporated into the model civil service law of the National Civil Service League as well as the National Municipal League; correspondingly, this policy flowered wherever merit systems were seriously applied. These developments did not go without their critics. Writing in 1909, Herbert Croly observed that "the civil service laws have been designed . . . to a very considerable extent for the purpose of protecting the subordinates against their chiefs; and that is scarcely to be conceived as a method of organizing administrative employees helpful to administrative efficiency."[18]

This significant change radically altered the function of the civil service commission. No longer did it serve simply to insure that political considerations did not prevail in public employment; it had gained the lawful right to review all the personnel actions of management. The original influentials of the civil service reform movement were dead set against this practice.[19] President Grover Cleveland, a considerable friend to civil service reform, felt that subjecting managers to a possible review of their removals was unwarranted. Accordingly, he wrote, "I am unwilling to . . . put officers of my own selection, in whom I have generally the utmost confidence . . . in a hampered, suspected, and discredited position."[20]

The civil service commissions with their new-found power of investigation and reinstatement had suddenly taken from management what had been its absolute prerogative: the right to fire an employee it deemed incompetent. Because of this development, almost all present-day disciplinary actions on the part of management are subject to a morass of administrative due process in a quasi-judicial setting. Such hearings are appropriately quasi-judicial because they are based upon a right of appeal mandated by legislation or provided for in a city charter or state constitution. Those hearing the appeal must take care that they conduct themselves with the detachment and deportment of the judiciary, for "decisions may be overturned by a court of law if the appellant's rights are not properly protected in the process."[21] While such hearings are not generally bound by the rules of evidence, their essential purpose, nevertheless, "is to determine if mitigating circumstances justify altering the proposed penalties."[22]

Reflective of the American legal tradition, government employees tend to be presumed innocent of incompetence until they are proven otherwise. Because this burden of proof is entirely upon management,[23] disciplinary actions are seldom entered into unless documented evidence is overwhelming and only then with great trepidation, for the manager is really putting himself and all his previous actions toward the employee in question on trial. This is a time-honored reluctance. As early as 1912 it was observed by

Charles A. Beard that municipal officials "would rather
permit their departmental work to remain unsatisfactory
than face the ordeal of wrangling in court or before a
board over the petty details which constitute an employee's inefficiency."[24] Attorneys representing employees
under charges have frequently succeeded "in turning the
hearings into a trial of the head of the department, instead of an appraisal of the charges against the employee."[25] Many a seemingly airtight case was lost because
what management may have considered irrelevant, the hearing officers later deemed mitigating circumstances. The
pathos of management's deteriorating situation was aptly
expressed by Herbert Kaufman: "Top management personnel
of the line agencies, their organizations now protected
against the raids of the spoilsmen, have begun to pray for
deliverance from their guardians."[26]

It has long been the opinion of the public personnel
apologists that "few jurisdictions do not have adequate
provision for forced separation when the work situation
demands it. If not enough workers are fired, it is probably for reasons other than the merit system."[27] What
nonsense! When the environment of the manager/employee
work situation in the public sector is examined in all its
subtlety, such a complaisant attitude toward the merit system as it typically functions can be shown to be unreasonable, illogical, and patently absurd. There is no more
pressing problem in managing the public service than the
increasing inability of the manager to control the work
situation. According to John W. Macy, Jr., Chairman of the
U.S. Civil Service Commission during the administrations
of presidents Kennedy and Johnson, "virtually every round-
table discussion of problems facing public managers will
quickly turn to the inability of the manager to discipline
nonproductive or insubordinate employees or to dismiss
those who have ceased to be productive or constitute
chronic supervisory problems."[28] Yet, when this writer
asked a recent bureau chief of the U.S. Civil Service
Commission why federal managers so frequently complain
that they are unable to rid themselves of the dead weight
in the organization, he replied, "I just don't accept that
argument. A federal manager can fire anyone he wants to;
but they're just too damn lazy to do the paperwork." This
sentiment is both widespread and valid. Although it is
true that the legal framework exists that allows managers
to dispose of incompetent and marginal employees, it has
long been recognized that a variety of significant factors
tend to mitigate against such action. It was observed by

Mosher and Kingsley in their 1936 text that the manager "may have the ultimate power of discharge so far as the law goes, but as the record of removals shows, he is not accustomed to use it because of attendant circumstances."[29] Listed below are eight such "attendant circumstances" of the present day.

1. It takes a tremendous amount of time to build up a case that will, in effect, stand up in court. While the organization may know that for years John Doe has been only half as productive as the other employees in his class, this has to be documented over a sustained period of time. The large number of managerial man-hours that have to go into building such a case is all too frequently an inhibitor of any action at all.

2. Even if this great investment of time and energy is undertaken, the eventual result is always a gamble. One never knows what mitigating circumstances the hearing officers may choose to recognize. The employee may still be suffering from shell shock that he received during World War II; or he may, to everybody's surprise, turn out to have a grandfather who was partly of Eskimo origin and proceed to seek redress for discrimination that he has suffered at the hands of management because of his new-found minority status; or his uncle might have gone to school with a congressman who is friendly with one of the civil service commissioners who, in turn, is inclined to "give the boy another chance." Remember, civil service commissioners may conduct themselves as, and have the integrity of, judges; but like judges they are the product of the political process and subject in one fashion or another to its pressures. Unfortunately, suggesting that a body of public officials possesses the collective integrity of the American judiciary is not a compliment.

3. Few things can kill an organization's morale so well as having within the work group an individual publicly proclaimed by management to be unworthy of his position, yet lingering on for month after month after month--possibly even retaining his position after the due process battle is over. In this latter situation, a management decision to initiate dismissal proceedings all over again is tantamount to persecution. The last thing that the organization needs is an incompetent martyr for other disgruntled employees to emulate. Organizational morale, like physical well-being, is always a most delicate balance. One therefore does not introduce malaise unless there is relative certainty that the eventual outcome will be benign.

4. Managers being individuals of a practical bent frequently see the advantage of transferring, or of allow-

ing a transfer of, a marginal employee to another segment
of the organization. "If you are an experienced administrator, you will never try to fire anybody--you will foist
him off on some unsuspecting colleague in another bureau,
or transfer him to the South Dakota field office."[30] This
solves one manager's problem by pushing it upon another.
Besides, a new work environment sometimes has a beneficial
effect on some employees. This process is certainly more
economical from the manager's point of view than formal
proceedings. Of course, if it is not possible to arrange
a transfer, the next best thing is to make the employee ineffectual within your own organization yet comfortable
enough so that he has no reason to complain. After all,
from the manager's position, it is frequently easier to
get an increased budget allocation for an additional employee than to seek to remove a wayward individual. While
such a tactic is on the surface a gross violation of the
responsibilities of the manager's position as well as the
public trust, this is a time-honored and very common gambit.

   5. All organizations possess a large degree of inertia, and this is especially true when it comes to the problem of removing people. All social organisms have a tendency to protect their inept members.[31] What better evidence is there of this than with performance reporting?
Management tigers all too frequently turn into pussycats
in order to avoid the embarrassing situation of dealing
with the poor performance of an employee.[32] In consequence,
efficiency ratings have tended to be a conspicuous failure.
In the federal service, for example, it has been reported
that almost everybody is given a satisfactory rating.[33]
If and when a manager decides to take action against an
employee, he is frequently faced with a number of years'
worth of satisfactory ratings. In building his case
against the employee, he will undoubtedly have to explain
why an employee who had been performing satisfactorily for
so many years "suddenly" went bad. The poor administration
of the rating program tends to inhibit such actions. In
effect, the manager in a collective sense has been hung by
a noose of his own making.[34]

   6. One cannot ignore the unions. They exist only to
protect the jobs and work-related prerogatives of their
members. Any threat to their most basic need--jobs for
their members--will have them rattling their sabers as
loudly or discreetly as the situation warrants. Why should
a manager sour his union relationships over one miscreant
employee? Besides, the union has almost unlimited resources
for lawyer's fees, and so forth, to pit against the mana-

ger's already-overburdened staff and the limited talent available from the personnel office. Against such odds, why fight? Surely the salary of one unproductive employee is a low price to pay for harmonious union relations. But then what is to prevent that one from growing to be a significant portion of the total work force?

7. The dismissal of a marginal employee may do that individual excessive harm. It is one thing to fire a young man or woman who, after adjusting to the disturbance this causes in their lives, will eventually find another position. It is another matter altogether to fire a person who has reached the age where they are neither entitled to adequate pension benefits nor likely to gain another position of similar monetary reward. Consequently, there is a great and understandable laxity toward taking action against a whole horde of middle-aged marginal performers. The organization, it is felt, simply by retaining them for so many years, owes them something better than unemployment for the rest of their working lives. This phenomenon could descriptively be termed compassionate corruption.[35]

8. There is seldom adequate incentive for a line supervisor to be held accountable for his lack of punitive action toward deserving employees. Why should he risk creating a difficult interpersonal situation with his subordinates for some vague notion of the public interest? Unless there is some extraordinary pressure upon him for productivity, there is simply no incentive for him to take the hard action that is occasionally the duty of all managers. One writer, Charles S. Hyneman, seems to have made the definitive statement on the subject almost 25 years ago: "The principal reason why employees who are incompetent or otherwise objectionable stay in the federal service is that administrative officials are not under sufficient compulsion to run them down and get rid of them."[36] But there is a more subtle dimension to this question of accountability. The public manager is not, after all, the proprietor of his own small business; the actions or inactions of his employees, unless they exhibit some gross misconduct, do not directly affect his own interests. Why should he be the one manager in his jurisdiction to take the waste of public funds seriously enough to take concrete action? Does it not take an individual of intense ideological conviction to act upon his beliefs when all around him exhibit contrary attitudes? Before interfering with a system that tolerates marginally performing employees, a reasonable person would have to be sure of the legitimacy of his actions. Precedence creates legitimacy. To upset

what has evolved as the natural order of things may be socially and morally illegitimate while at the same time being legally appropriate.[37]

All the above factors tend to mitigate against managers undertaking disciplinary or removal actions. While state and local jurisdictions vary in their degree of protection for employees, it is reasonable to imply that whenever a strong merit system exists, procedural safeguards tend to undermine the authority of managers. Even O. Glenn Stahl has admitted that "some of the more recent merit-system laws in state and local government show little sign of avoiding the traps of over proceduralization. A few have gone so far as to make discipline almost impossible."[38]

One cannot deal with the subject of procedural safeguards for public employees without delving into several questions of value. Are all these discipline-inhibiting safeguards really necessary? Why should the managers not have the absolute discretion to discharge employees for other than religious or political reasons as the original reformers envisioned? The essential question here is one common to American jurisprudence: Is it more desirable to chance having one person treated unjustly or to provide for due process procedures that may allow many individuals to escape punitive sanctions? The whole thrust of the recent Supreme Court rulings on the procedural rights of criminal suspects has been to strengthen the procedural rights of individuals at the expense of the discretion of law enforcement agencies.[39] Just as the job of the policeman has been made more difficult by the Supreme Court's expansion of constitutional safeguards, the task of public managers has been made grossly more complicated by the expansion of the procedural rights of public employees. In each instance these expansions were the direct result of past abuses of discretion. Just as the theoretical foundations of the American legal system prefers to allow guilty men to go free rather than chance the conviction of an innocent individual, American civil service merit systems at all levels of government prefer to retain their marginal and incompetent employees rather than risk doing an injustice to an individual. And so it should be in a democracy. Yet life is not as neat as all this. Even within this elaborate system of procedural safeguards, abuses occur.[40] But they are minor compared to the vast amount of protection that procedural due process affords the public employee. While the protection of due process is being discussed mainly with regard to incompetent employees, the overly or supercompetent employee is frequently just as much in need of this protection. According to Laurence J. Peter, author of <u>The Peter Principle</u>, super-competence is even more objectionable than incompetence. Because supercompetents have a tendency to disrupt the traditional hierarchy, their actions often lead to unwarranted dismissal proceedings.[41]

Those who have fought hardest for these safeguards over the years--the employees themselves, their union representatives, and politicians who saw electoral support in the issue--tend to respond to the hamstringing of management's traditional prerogatives with the "there is no such thing as a bad boy" argument. If the organization suffers from inhibited productivity, the fault lies not in ourselves, but rather in our managers. Considering that most of the public management corps--the lower and middle levels-- benefits from the same protective cocoon as does the rank and file, there is a thriving germ of truth in this allegation. Managers at all levels in all jurisdictions find themselves in an almost untenable position. They can neither urge their charges on to greater productive heights nor effectively impose sanctions of sufficient weight to frighten workers into productive acts. With their backs collectively to the wall, public managers have no real choice of action; they must learn to manage. While this may seem a facile answer, its seriousness become evident upon further examination.

Several of the more serious authors of important books dealing with the broader concepts of the American civil service have found it convenient for purposes of analysis to organize the evolution of public personnel practices into transition periods.[42] The implementation of Jacksonian democracy and the advent of the reform movement are two of the more obvious phases of historical transition. Both of these transitions were essentially those of power --one political faction assuming office at the direct expense of another--although higher motives were invariably proclaimed. Today we are in the midst of a transition that is radically different in dimension. Because of all the factors previously enumerated in this discussion, life tenure has been effectively achieved by great numbers of civil service employees. Happily, not all employees take advantage of this, and the degree of turnover is roughly comparable to that of private industry.[43] But generally speaking only those comparatively few employees who have grossly violated the norms of conduct of their peer group are ever formally dismissed. Where does this situation lead? Now that public managers are finding themselves increasingly "boxed in" with employees of mixed motivations and attitudes toward their work, they have no real choice but to work with what they have. With the managerial luxury of discharging a poor or marginal performer rapidly disappearing, there is a newfound impetus to have the managerial applications of the behavioral sciences fill this disciplinary void. While the managerial techniques of job design and organizational development are still in a primitive and experimental stage, private industry has already experienced substantial successes.[44] Public managers feeling themselves left with nothing but bluster as a managerial tool must turn increasingly in this direction. The transition will be achieved when life tenure is no longer viewed so much as an obstacle to managerial effectiveness, but as an opportunity to develop each employee to his fullest potential.

NOTES

1. Woodrow Wilson, "The Study of Administration," in Peter Woll, ed., Public Administration and Policy (New York: Harper & Row, 1966), p. 29. Wilson's essay originally appeared in Political Science Quarterly, vol. 2 (June 1887).

2. Herbert Kaufman, "Emerging Conflicts in the Doctrines of Public Administration," American Political Science Review 50 (December 1956): 1057-73.

3. More than a decade after Kaufman's original presentation, he reaffirms the vitality and desirability of "neutral competence." Herbert Kaufman, "Administrative Decentralization and Political Powers," Public Administration Review 29 (January/February 1969): 3-15.

4. Henry Bruere, New City Government (New York: D. Appleton, 1913), p. 119.

5. Carl Russell Fish, The Civil Service and the Patronage (New York: Russell & Russell, 1904, 1963), p. 233. Fish's views were reflected by a number of his contemporaries. A rather scathing example is provided by Thomas C. Devlin, who found that the merit system "is accompanied by an emasculation of character, a complete loss of patriotism, and a lack of husbandry that is appalling." Municipal Reform in the United States (New York: G. P. Putnam's Sons, 1896), p. 100. Similar sentiments are still echoed today. According to Holtan P. Odegard, "civil service regulations, which originally began as antidotes to political patronage . . . have since tended toward feather-

bedding protectionism." The Politics of Truth: Toward Reconstruction in Democracy (University: University of Alabama Press, 1971), p. 346. James C. Charlesworth has written that "merit systems attract many security-minded and mousey weaklings." Governmental Administration (New York: Harper & Bros., 1951), p. 442. One can only speculate what "mousey" means!

6. Municipal Manpower Commission, Governmental Manpower for Tomorrow's Cities (New York: McGraw-Hill, 1962), p. 60.

7. Ibid., pp. 64-68.

8. For a discussion of the implementation of position classification programs, see Jay M. Shafritz, Position Classification: A Behavioral Analysis for the Public Service (New York: Praeger, 1973), pp. 13-22.

9. William Seal Carpenter, The Unfinished Business of Civil Service Reform (Princeton: Princeton University Press, 1952), pp. 45-46.

10. Paul P. Van Riper, History of the United States Civil Service (Evanston, Ill.: Row, Peterson & Co., 1958), p. 102. Van Riper's source for Curtis' statement is Ruth M. Berens, "Blueprint for Reform: Curtis, Easton, and Schurz" (Master's thesis, Department of Political Science, University of Chicago, 1943), p. 50.

11. Leonard D. White, The Republican Era: A Study in Administrative History: 1869-1901 (New York: The Free Press, 1958), p. 341.

12. Frank Mann Stewart, The National Civil Service Reform League: History, Activities, and Problems (Austin: University of Texas, 1929), p. 207. The league expanded its resolution in 1889 to say:

> While fully recognizing that the absolute power of removal must be vested in the appointing power subject only to a sound discretion, the League holds that the system of making removals upon secret charges or specified acts preferred by unknown accusers, without opportunity for explanation or denial, is inquisitorial in its character, unjust in its results, and like the spoils system itself, repugnant to the spirit of American institutions.

13. White, The Republican Era, pp. 344-45.

14. Commission on Organization of the Executive Branch of the Government, Task Force Report on Personnel and Civil Service (Washington, D.C.: U.S. Government Printing Office, 1955), p. 95.

15. The appeal rights of nonveterans were made equal to those of veterans by an executive order of President Kennedy.

16. Lewis Meriam, Personnel Administration in the Federal Government (Washington, D.C.: Brookings Institution, 1937), p. 2.

17. Carpenter, The Unfinished Business of Civil Service Reform, p. 115.

18. Herbert Croly, The Promise of American Life (New York: Macmillan, 1909), p. 335.

19. Stewart, The National Civil Service Reform League, pp. 206-07.

20. White, The Republican Era, pp. 343-44.

21. Winston W. Crouch, Guide for Modern Personnel Commissions (Chicago: International Personnel Management Association, 1973), p. 58.

22. Ibid.

23. This was not always the case. "An interesting feature of the trial board method as practiced in Chicago during the years when that city led the country in civil service administration was that the Civil Service Commission itself, through its secretary, preferred charges against employees when their efficiency rating fell below acceptable standards. In other words, the Commission sought not only to protect employees against unjust removal, but also to rid the service of employees whose efficiency did not warrant their retention, even though the appointing officers themselves did not take the initiative in bringing those employees to trial." William C. Beyer, "Municipal Civil Service in the United States," in Carl J. Friedrich et al., Problems of the American Public Service (New York: McGraw-Hill, 1935), p. 131.

24. Charles Beard, American City Government (New York: The Century Co., 1912), p. 116.

25. Charles R. Adrian and Charles Press, Governing Urban America, 4th ed. (New York: McGraw-Hill, 1972), p. 366.

26. Herbert Kaufman, "The Growth of the Federal Personnel System," in Francis E. Rourke, ed., Bureaucratic Power in National Politics, 2d ed. (Boston: Litte, Brown & Co., 1972), p. 269.

27. O. Glenn Stahl, Public Personnel Administration, 5th ed. (New York: Harper & Row, 1962), p. 373. In fairness to Stahl it should be pointed out that his opinions on this subject changed considerably with the sixth edition (1971) of his text. Winston Crouch, however, remains unrepentant, stating in his 1973 book that it is a "folklore belief that civil service 'freezes' employees into the

work force." Crouch, <u>Guide for Modern Personnel Commissions</u>, p. 66.

28. John W. Macy, Jr., <u>Public Service: The Human Side of Government</u> (New York: Harper & Row, 1971), p. 20.

29. William E. Mosher and J. Donald Kingsley, <u>Public Personnel Administration</u> (New York: Harper & Bros, 1936), p. 48.

30. John Fischer, "Let's Go Back to the Spoils System," in Dwight Waldo, ed., <u>Ideas and Issues in Public Administration</u> (New York: McGraw-Hill, 1953), p. 201.

31. For an excellent analysis of this as it regards the work situation, see William J. Goode, "The Protection of the Inept," <u>American Sociological Review</u>, vol. 32 (February 1967).

32. Andrew H. Cochran, "Management Tigers and Pussycats," <u>Personnel Journal</u> 50 (December 1971): 924-26. Douglas McGregor agreed with Cochran's pussycat phenomenon while not calling it such. "An Uneasy Look at Performance Appraisal," <u>Harvard Business Review</u> 50 (September-October 1972): 133-38.

33. Mary S. Schinagl, <u>History of Efficiency Ratings in the Federal Government</u> (New York: Bookman Associates, 1966), p. 87.

34. Or, in Elizabethan prose, "hoist on one's own petard." See also William Shakespeare, <u>Hamlet</u>, Act III, Scene 4.

35. Carl J. Friedrich would call this the "functionality of corruption." <u>The Pathology of Politics</u> (New York: Harper & Row, 1972), p. 157. Friedrich notes that it is the corruption of the bureaucracy that facilitates humane decision making. It was the corruption of the German and Russian bureaucracies during the 1930s that saved many lives that would otherwise have been lost to the terrors of the period (p. 130). The limited corruption of American bureaucracies is similar in degree but vastly different in scope.

36. Charles S. Hyneman, <u>Bureaucracy in a Democracy</u> (New York: Harper & Bros., 1950), p. 409.

37. For a further discussion of organizational legitimacy, see Edgar H. Schein and Gorden L. Lippitt, "Supervisory Attitudes Toward the Legitimacy of Influencing Subordinates," Journal of Applied Behavioral Science 2 (April/May/June 1966): 199-209.

38. O Glenn Stahl, <u>Public Personnel Administration</u>, 6th ed. (New York: Harper & Row, 1971), p. 317.

39. Some of the major Supreme Court decisions in this area are <u>Mallory</u> v. <u>United States</u>, 354 U.S. 449 (1957);

Mapp v. Ohio, 367 U.S. 643 (1961); Gideon v. Wainwright, 372 U.S. 335 (1963); Escobedo v. Illinois, 378 U.S. 1 (1964); Miranda v. Arizona, 384 U.S. 436 (1966).

40. An excellent accounting of some of these is given in Robert Vaughn, The Spoiled System (Washington, D.C.: Public Interest Research Group, 1972). This is the study of the federal civil service sponsored by Ralph Nader.

41. Peter calls such dismissals "hierarchial exfoliation." For further analysis as well as horrible examples, see Laurence J. Peter and Raymond Hull, The Peter Principle (New York: Bantam Books, 1970), pp. 26-31.

42. For examples see Mosher, Democracy and the Public Service; and Van Riper, History of the United States Civil Service.

43. "In spite of the dearth of turnover data on public jurisdictions in general, such information as exists suggests that turnover in government employment is at least as low as in most private employment." Stahl, Public Personnel Administration, 6th ed., p. 329.

44. The best summary of the success of these programs is the Report of a Special Task Force to the Secretary of Health, Education and Welfare, Work in America (Cambridge, Mass.: The Massachusetts Institute of Technology Press, 1973).

CHAPTER

4

POSITION MANAGEMENT:
A CONCEPTUAL FRAMEWORK
FOR PERSONNEL
ADMINISTRATION

Before the specific problems of managing and motivating employees in the tenured environment of the public service can be considered, the implications and dimensions of
managerial philosophy must be assayed. All organizations
are guided by a philosophy of management. It may be stated
or unstated, conscious or unconscious, advertent or inad-
vertent; but it is always there. No management program
can be viable without a guiding philosophy and the behavioral techniques necessary for implementing that philosophy.
A philosophy could be as simplistic as Henry Ford's famous
dictum: "All that we ask of the men is that they do the
work which is set before them"; or as sophisticated as that
used by the Polaroid Corporation, where meaningful and fulfilling work for its employees is a "central and explicit
goal of the organization."[1] In the first instance there
was an underlying assumption that employees not responding
adequately to the "work which is set before them" would be
dismissed. The behavioral technique used here is as simple as that applied to those small experimental animals
who have spent generations running mazes for psychologists.
In this kind of managerial atmosphere, the employee tends
to be viewed "as an inert instrument performing the tasks
assigned to him."[2] Under these conditions "there is a
tendency to view personnel as a given rather than as a
variable in the system."[3] In the second instance, the underlying assumptions are radically different. The organization has assumed a responsibility for providing meaningful and fulfilling work for its employees in addition to
mere wages, the rationale being that such a strategy is
more conducive to high productivity. Just as religion defines an individual's attitude toward life, a managerial

philosophy defines management's attitude toward work. Management by the exercise of its philosophy earns, in turn, a reciprocal attitude on the part of the work force toward their responsibilities.

Personnel actions in any organization derive their legitimacy and direction from management's philosophy toward the work force. That an operating philosophy is not written or otherwise formally stated is irrelevant to its existence. An organization must have a philosophy or conceptual framework that facilitates the decision-making process. After all, management's prime responsibility is decision making in support of the organizational mission. Managers must have a benchmark by which to function. "A philosophy of management, understood and applied by the entire management group, provides this benchmark. It also acts as a frame of reference for the facilitation of communications; it provides normative consensus."[4] Without such a philosophy or normative consensus, the individual or groups constituting the factions of the organization will operate without an overall integration of thought and corresponding action. Such a condition amounts to management by mild chaos. Actually, many jurisdictions have commendable managerial philosophies. Ream upon ream of paper has been dedicated to espousing an official view of what an idyllic place the jurisdiction is in which to work. The only problem with these fine-sounding philosophies is that they are seldom operational; they tend to exist only on paper. When subordinates perceive the reality of the situation, there is an understandable tendency toward "frustration and cynicism about top management's pretensions."[5]

One might think that the primary managerial task would be to define the organizational mission. Then a managerial philosophy could accommodate itself to the exigencies of the situation. Different philosophies are appropriate to different organizational environments and work situations. The philosophy appropriate to a military combat unit would hardly be suitable for a research program in solid-state physics. Unfortunately, the environments of public sector personnel programs mitigate against the development of a coherent managerial philosophy.[6] The most basic reasons for this are external to the nature of the individuals constituting the organization. While private organizations typically exist in response to a specific goal, the objectives of public organizations are seldom as definite. It has frequently been shown that the professed objectives of a public organization are only vaguely related to its ac-

tual mission. For example, the goals of correctional institutions and mental hospitals may be therapeutic, but
the organizations' specific mission is more likely to be
simply that of detention.[7] The goal of a police department may be to enforce all the laws of the community, but
its specific mission is more likely to be the maintenance
of public order.[8] One goal of a public personnel unit may
be to find the best qualified managers for its agency, but
its specific mission may be limited to processing the pa-
pers of those candidates with prior political clearance.
When the public policy process is so schizophrenic, it is
little wonder that coherent managerial philosophies find
it difficult or impossible to emerge.[9]

How can a personnel policy premised on one set of
rhetorical conditions be implemented in a real world operating on contradictory premises? It is a gross understate-
ment to assert that this aspect of public personnel management tends to hinder severely the development of comprehensive managerial strategies and objectives. This is one of
the reasons why management by objectives has not made significant inroads in public personnel operations.[10] There
are seldom true objectives in public personnel administration; only expediencies. It has even been suggested that
the personnel director might be more aptly titled the "personnel reactor."[11] The political environment is such that
actual organizational objectives can sometimes not even be
stated to the personnel unit's own employees. While top
management well knows that one of its prime responsibilities
is the foisting of politicos upon the career civil service,
this fact is never mentioned in the personnel unit's annual
report or various public relations releases. All organizational objectives in government tend to be inherently unstable in reaction to the dynamics of the political process.[12]

Because of this institutionalized incapacity to have
set objectives, public personnel operations have tended to
be haphazard affairs. The whims of politics--both of the
organizational and party variety--the constraints of antiquated operating mandates, and the immaturity of public
personnel practice as a profession have long conspired to
make the level of sophistication of personnel operations
at all levels of governmental organizations more a function
of chance than of purposeful design. Except for pulling
people into and occasionally pushing people out of the organization, the personnel unit has typically not tended to
be of significant assistance in the accomplishment of an
agency's mission. On the contrary, many a top-level admin-

istrator could argue persuasively that the personnel department with its rituals and obtuse methods is more of a
hindrance than anything else. The examining process is
an excellent example of this. Obviously an examinations
program is the backbone of any merit system. However, research reported by two former assistants in the New York
City mayor's office provides devastating proof of the in-
anity of the examining process as it typically operates.
According to E. S. Savas and Sigmund G. Ginsburg, the examinations system "discriminates against those applicants
who are most qualified according to its own standards,"[13]
because candidates with the lower test scores are more
likely to be hired than candidates with higher grades.
Their study of a representative sample of written examinations showed that the lower the percentile ranking of a candidate, the more likely it was that he would be hired.
The main reason for this is the inherent delay, usually
many months, between the taking of an examination and the
tendering of an actual job offer. In the interim, those
candidates most able to find other job opportunities did
so. As one might expect, those able to obtain other positions were usually the candidates who attained the higher
scores on the written exam. If it is maintained that this
finding, while true, is irrelevant, that the hundredth person on a list of eligibles is not significantly worse than
those taken from the top, "then one is essentially admit-
ting that the entire examination process is virtually useless."[14]

The critics have not been kind to the rituals of the
civil service examining process. "Rules of one," whereby
the highest scoring person on an eligible list is the only
one that can be hired, are not any less absurd because
they are common. Meticulously computing examination scores
to three decimal places may provide personnel technicians
with a smug sense of assurance in the validity of their
calculations, "but its relevance to the identification of
merit may be more akin to the theological disputations as
to how many angels can dance on the head of a pin."[15]
Critiques of personnel operations typically conclude that
personnel operatives "seem enmeshed in programs, tools and
techniques for their own sake. Creative energy is focused
primarily on improving mechanics . . . which may or may not
be effective means to achieve the ends being served."[16]
This phenomenon is a rather typical psychosis of organizational functionaries. Not having a professional orientation, the functionary exhibits "a trained incapacity to
deal with problems . . . in substantive rather than func-

tional terms."[17] Thomas H. Patten, Jr. has noted that personnel "often has a peculiar bureaucratic will of its own" wherein the operatives are so specialized in their "trivial expertise" that they "become a mutual admiration society, patting themselves on the back, complimenting the most useless among them as good technicians."[18] Patten observes rather sarcastically that the personnelists' "favorite activity is the hallmark of every moribund organization, namely, they enact the last drama of a dying organization by rewriting the rule book."[19] This unhealthy situation with its attendant institutionalized degree of conflict between personnel and the line managers exists to some extent in practically all jurisdictions.

While a limited amount of conflict is frequently healthy and to be encouraged in an organization,[20] the personnel department is usually not involved with the creative tension of competition, but rather with a battle of conflicting ideologies that is more likely to generate mutual contempt than mutual respect. Since line managers are of necessity mission oriented, it is understandable that they are not sympathetic to the frequently unreasonable constraints that the personnel department would impose upon them in the name of the civil service system, merit staffing, or of some equally righteous-sounding phrase. This conflict of roles must be mitigated before these two contending factions can act in concert. Conflict is usually resolved by a process of mutual accommodation. But since personnel departments are almost invariably in a weaker organizational position than important line components, they must take the first step toward accommodation. The personnelists must isolate and eventually eliminate those rigid minds whose battle cry might well be "the merit system, right or wrong"; for they have gratuitously brought the contempt of top management down upon this total group of otherwise well-meaning aspiring professionals. In consequence, the newest approaches in human resources management have been assigned, frequently by default, to other organizational units; or more likely, simply ignored. Only when personnel develops a complementary rather than an antagonistic role will the public personnel unit return itself from its largely self-imposed exile from the mainstream of the management process.

A new role set for public personnel departments that responds to this need for a complementary posture has been gradually evolving. In recognition of the fact that the problems of managing the human resources of an organization must be approached comprehensively, an increasing number of personnel departments, notably in private industry and certain federal agencies, have begun to take an expansive view of their mandate. Instead of viewing the personnel function as simply that collection of disparate duties necessary to recruit, pay, and discharge employees, they assume their appropriate mission to be the maximum utilization of their organization's human resources. There has been some success at appropriating this new function for two basic reasons. First, the maximum utilization of an organization's human resources, like economy and efficiency, is a goal that, while unattainable, can hardly be denied by top administrators. Second, while other organizational units have operating responsibilities, there seldom exists in public organizations a unit specifically accountable for the maximum development of its human capital.[21] The personnel department can fill this void if it has the will. In doing so it can not only revitalize many segments of its host organization; it can also metamorphose itself from a sophisticated clerical or low-level professional operation into an in-house group of behavioral consultants with ongoing housekeeping functions. This role set will reduce the cost of the parent organization's operations as well as have a revolutionary effect on the content, processes, and personnel of the public personnel profession.

The greatest difficulty antecedent to this role set revolution lies in conceptualizing the most basic personnel task. It is as difficult to get a handle on maximizing human resources as it is on increasing the effectiveness of the agency's programs. Both are broad nebulous goals that by their nature cannot be fully achieved. An organization can only strive toward them. It is precisely because the goals are so vague that it is so difficult to know how to approach the problem. This is where the concept of position management can be invaluable. As a conceptual framework it can help define problems and point out avenues to solutions. Used properly it can bring a semblance of order to events and situations that would otherwise be paralyzingly confusing. Position management, by suggesting a logical and orderly means to approach the orchestration of an organization's human resources, is an invaluable aid in defining and resolving personnel problems concerning employee motivation, productivity, job design, morale, and a variety of related problems. Generally, position management is a useful rubric under which to hang the array of information on the work situation provided by the behavioral sciences. Specifically, position management calls for the analysis of an organization's work to assure that it relates meaningfully to the agency's mission, and for the making of decisions on organizational structure and job design that will insure the most advantageous use of the organization's manpower. One must beware of thinking of this as simply arranging for the most efficient use of the workers in the tradition of the old scientific management school of thought.[22] While a procedure may be the most physically efficient means of accomplishing a given task, such other factors as internal motivation and peer group pressures have long been shown to be far more influential in determining eventual output. A modern position management purview takes into account all of the exigencies of the work situation.

As a conceptual tool, position management permits a manager to think diagnostically about personnel resource problems. By examining a problem situation in light of behavioral findings on organizational dynamics or with the aid of a behavioral consultant, the manager can perceive a logical course of action. The public sector has long been exceedingly good about the "hygiene" factors of the work situation--working conditions, salary, vacations, sick leave, and so on.[23] Now with the advent of militant employee unions, this seems to be an increasing trend. Correspondingly, however, the public sector has been grossly negligent about the motivational aspects of public employment, perhaps naively assuming that patriotism, civic pride, or party loyalty would compensate for managerial skill. Too often personnel problems are resolved by the simple expedient of hiring more employees instead of looking at the root causes of low productivity and its attendant conditions.

The low productivity of governmental employees seems to occupy as prominent a place in American folklore as does the crooked politician. Perhaps the prevalent nature of such folk wisdom is due in both cases to a healthy germ of truth. Crooked politicians notwithstanding, there is ample evidence of the low productivity of the civil service. In Chicago a recent investigation found that "highway-department maintenance men regularly devote the first hour of their work day to eating breakfast."[24] An investigation of New York City employees found that water meter readers read on the average less than half as many meters as private sector counterparts; that truck drivers delivering supplies to city agencies only worked about half a day; that building inspectors tended to take off at least a third of a day; and that welfare caseworkers--being college

graduates and of a more intellectual bent--were observed
playing chess or reading for several hours at a time.[25]
A college senior wanting to "vent some frustration after a
summer of incredible boredom" wrote a letter to the Washington Post in which she confessed, "I spent about one
hour a day engaged in actual work, and the remaining seven
were spent writing letters or reading. About the only
good thing to come out of my summer's employment was the
fact that I read, on the average, a book a day."[26] News-
paper columnist Marianne Means, curious about the paraly-
sis that Watergate was alleged to be causing in the federal
government, interviewed a mid-level bureaucrat in the Department of Commerce who, after telling her of his daily
hours with assorted newspapers, magazines, and books, declared, "One thing Watergate and Nixon are doing for this
government; they are producing the best read public servants in history."[27]

To be sure, the above examples are not representative
of the majority of American civil service employees; but
they are not so unusual that they can be dismissed as isolated instances. While the author assumes that a majority
of public employees are conscientious, even dedicated to
their jobs, the productivity of a healthy minority is well
below any reasonable standard. It seems reasonable to hypothesize that this marginally productive minority is about
evenly divided between those who actively seek to "steal"
time and those who are indolent because of management's
failure to supervise and motivate them properly. Skepti-
cal readers are invited to spend a few weeks at the middle
or lower levels of almost any large jurisdiction.

Such administrative sloppiness can no longer be tolerated in the face of increasing budget squeezes. A congressional commission recently proposed legislation that
would allow the federal government to contract-out previously in-house manpower functions if they could be performed more economically by outside private sources.[28]
Richard Croker was a Tammany boss of the last century who
supposedly gained $5 million at the public's expense. Ac-
cording to former officials of New York City's finance administration, "Croker couldn't steal in a year what is lost
in a month of municipal ineptitude. For instance, it costs
the city about $42 a ton to pick up garbage while private
cartmen charge about $28 a ton for the same service."[29]
Increased productivity by public employees may be this nation's last great untapped source of public revenue. The
only way to tap this source is through increasing the motivational qualities of government jobs by means of a position management program.

While it is necessarily concerned with manpower planning,[30] staffing patterns, and career lines, the essence
of a position management program is job design. Its most
basic strategy is to design jobs that are self-motivating,
to create work situations where the employee is both more
productive and content to be so. The payoff for a successful program is obviously enormous. Productivity goes up,
and turnover and absenteeism go dramatically down. A HEW
Task Force Report, Work in America, concluded that the redesign of jobs holds out "some promise to decrease mental
and physical health costs, increase productivity, and improve the quality of life for millions of Americans at all
occupational levels."[31] The essential task is to blend
the right mix of organizational structure and work assign-
ments into an intrinsically motivating situation. Employees motivated by the nature of their work tend to be more
productive than those motivated merely to retain their
jobs. Thus, an organization achieving its mission with X
number of employees motivated merely to retain their jobs
can achieve that same mission with X minus Y number of employees if they are highly motivated. Creating work situations that enhance the motivational qualities of the work
itself has proven to be a successful tactic in many of the
largest private corporations.[32] While all federal departments have been required to have comprehensive position
management programs since 1965,[33] this has been interpreted
by most departments to mean position control, essentially
a budgetary procedure having nothing to do with the design
of jobs. A few agencies have even published some position
management and/or job design materials; but such publica-
tions are not necessarily indicative of ongoing programs.[34]

A position management program, having to constantly
cross the many jurisdictional boundaries in a large organization, is of necessity an interdisciplinary undertaking.
Neither the personnel department nor any given line division can possibly have within itself all the disparate
skills essential for a comprehensive program. Even the
most sophisticated job design authority cannot tell a supervisor of technical experts how to best organize the tasks
for which he is responsible. Thus, the role of a job design expert is frequently restricted to that of an adviser.
Task design considerations must obviously be secondary to
technical constraints. The most competent and experienced
job design expert is helpless without the active cooperation of the line managers. Even if the jobs under study
required only slight and easily mastered skills, active
line management cooperation would be essential; the success-

ful implementation of any new work procedures is almost
totally dependent upon their cooperation. The personnel
department can beg and cajole, but unless line managers
are enthusiastic about a program, it has no practical
chance of success. In recognition of this reality, the
team approach to position management has evolved as the
best means to mobilize an array of skills to tackle a problem situation and to elicit the cooperation of the formal
as well as the informal influences upon the organization's
effectiveness. A position management program creates the
formal situation wherein an interdisciplinary effort is not
only feasible, but legitimatized as well.

Position management teams by their nature are assembled on an ad hoc basis to deal with a previously identified problem, such as high error rates, constant bottle-
necks, or poor morale. The team is organized by a facilitator, usually a member of the personnel staff. While the
facilitator may be from a management analysis section or
other unit, he must have at least a basic knowledge of job
design and a rudimentary familiarity with the social
science research on employee motivation. His primary task
is to translate behavioral findings into practical position
management approaches for the particular organizational
unit under study. Practical approaches, having to reflect
the organizational culture and the realities of power relationships, must vary with the circumstances. The facilitator will not be able simply to apply textbook solutions
to easily recognizable problems; he must be imaginative
enough to modify standard techniques and procedures to fit
the unique environment of the organization with which he
is working.

After a preliminary overview of the problem, the other
members of the team are chosen by the facilitator in con-
sultation with appropriate organizational influentials.
Team members are selected either because of their special
skills--for example, a classifier if a classification problem is involved, a technical expert if such advice is needed
--or because of their political position in the organization. For example, it may be desirable to have the supervisor of the work unit under study on the team because of
his special technical skill; but he is more likely to be
put on the team because of his pivotal political position
with respect to the implementation of the team's eventual
recommendations. If the supervisor concerned or other persons in similar positions of organizational clout or en-
trenchment is not co-opted into the position management
decisional process, there is the likelihood of a nonenthu-

siastic or even downright hostile attitude toward the eventual action recommendations of the team. Supervisors are frequently both resistant and fearful of programs that seek to alter the duties of their subordinates, feeling that such changes either threaten or adversely reflect upon their own position.[35] Union opposition to such programs is also common, but this usually can be resolved if the program is a sincere attempt to make the work situation more palatable and if employee groups or union representatives are in on every phase of the program.[36]

The ultimate size of the team is dependent upon the size of the work unit under study, the expertise required to resolve the problem, and--with an eye to implementation --the realities of organizational politics. The role of the facilitator is to assemble the team according to the above criteria, function as the executive officer if not the formal leader of the group, and serve as the team's consultant on job design and the motivational aspects of work. No matter how well-trained a facilitator may be, he will be limited in his ability to function as an in-house consultant both by the limits of his skill with position management and by his continuing involvement with the organization. A good facilitator should be able to recognize when he reaches the extremes of his substantive and/or political skills; at such a point an outside consultant may be essential.

Position management has all too frequently been confused with and compared to position classification; yet classification is always a subordinate function in a viable position management program. While many classifiers are adept at job design, the classification process itself is usually neutral on the content of jobs, being only concerned with the appropriate duties and responsibilities for the sake of legal justifications and salary scales. In contrast, position management deals with the whole panoply of the work situation. It differs from organization development mainly by taking a micro rather than a macro approach to an organizational problem. Each assumes that an organization exists both internally and externally in a dynamic, constantly evolving environment to which the organization must adapt or become ineffectual. Once an organization has been developed into an effective productive entity, it is a comprehensive position management program that will maintain this effectiveness and stave off the need for a massive and traumatic organizational development effort.[37]

The absolute necessity for effective position management programs and other behavioral science organizational interventions will radically alter the role of the public personnel practitioner in the future. The present accounting and policing functions will gradually give way to an in-house consulting team specializing in the motivation and optimal utilization of its human resources. But this is hardly the case now. Personnel departments generally have well-earned reputations for not having "aggressively kept pace with the developing knowledge and behavior skills that future line managers are acquiring."[38] Unless personnel makes some hasty efforts to revitalize and professionalize itself, it is safe to predict that other organizational units of behavioral scientists will be created to fill this void, and the downgrading of the personnel function will be formally accomplished.[39]

While this discussion has spoken to the future, present realities are a much less optimistic matter. The ensuing chapters will concern themselves with the question of why public personnel agencies have not taken a more expansive and professional view of their responsibilities.

NOTES

1. For a discussion of Polaroid's program, see William F. Dowling, Jr., and Leonard R. Sayles, How Managers Motivate: The Imperatives of Supervision (New York: McGraw-Hill, 1971), pp. 30-31.

2. James G. March and Herbert A. Simon, Organizations (New York: Wiley, 1958), p. 29.

3. Ibid.

4. Billy J. Hodge and Herbert J. Johnson, Management and Organizational Behavior: A Multidimensional Approach (New York: Wiley, 1970), p. 44.

5. Paul Pigors and Charles A. Myers, Personnel Administration: A Point of View and a Method (New York: McGraw-Hill, 1969), p. 60. This situation is no less common in the private sector, as this short case study illustrates. "This organization has a written policy stating the frequency of merit reviews and increases. One of its managers noted that when his time for review arrived, nothing happened. When he recommended action after review of his subordinates, delays always occurred. When he finally asked his superior about these dalays he was told it was their policy. In other words, it was the policy to disregard policy in the matter of raises based on merit review. The organization saves a lot of money this way, he was told." Charles D. Flory and R. Alec Mackenzie,

The Credibility Gap in Management (New York: Van Nostrand
Reinhold Co., 1971), p. 11.

6. This absence of a guiding management philosophy
for personnel administration has until recently been
equally true for the private sector. For a discussion of
the personnel philosophies exhibited by American business,
see Charles R. Milton, Ethics and Expediency in Personnel
Management: A Critical History of Personnel Philosophy
(Columbia: University of South Carolina Press, 1970).

7. Amitai Etzioni, "Two Approaches to Organizational
Analysis: A Critique and a Suggestion," Administrative
Science Quarterly 5 (September 1960): 263. "Public goals
fail to be realized not because of poor planning, unantici-
pated consequences, or hostile environment. They are not
meant to be realized" (p. 260).

8. This is supported by James Q. Wilson, Varieties
of Police Behavior: The Management of Law and Order in
Eight Communities (Cambridge: Harvard University Press,
1968).

9. "Government agencies present a unique challenge
to the manager, in many cases, just to discover (or de-
cipher) the main objective of the agency." Thomas P.
Kleber, "The Six Hardest Areas to Manage by Objectives,"
Personnel Journal 51 (August 1972): 574.

10. For a private sector analysis, see George S.
Odiorne, Personnel Administration by Objectives (Homewood,
Ill.: Richard D. Irwin, 1971).

11. Stephen M. Sweeney, "Squaw-Man in the Personnel
Department?" Personnel Journal 51 (December 1972): 888.

12. The literature on management by objectives in the
public sector is scant. Some recent examples are Walter
Baker, "Management by Objectives: A Philosophy and Style
of Management for the Public Sector," Canadian Public Administration 12 (Fall 1969): 427-43; Rodney H. Brady, "MBO
Goes to Work in the Public Sector," Harvard Business Review 51 (March-April 1973): 65-74; Dale D. McConkey, "Applying Management by Objectives to Non-Profit Organizations," S.A.M. Advanced Management Journal 38 (January
1973): 10-20.

13. E. S. Savas and Sigmund G. Ginsburg, "The Civil
Service: A Meritless System," Public Interest 32 (Summer
1973): p. 76.

14. Ibid., p. 77. Robert W. Galloway views this loss
of the best-qualified applicants as a Gresham's Law of
personnel in operation. "By a preoccupation with assuring
equal treatment and fairness to all we drive out or lose
the talented or the exceptional person." Robert W. Gallo-

way, <u>Public Personnel Administration: Critique and Credo</u>
(Chicago: Public Personnel Association, Public Employee
Relations Library no. 21, 1970), p. 20.

15. Galloway, <u>Public Personnel Administration</u>, p. 11.

16. Elean M. Volante, "Are Personnel People Functioning as Tinkerers or Professionals?" <u>Management of Personnel Quarterly</u> 4 (Summer 1965): 28.

17. F. William Howton, <u>Functionaries</u> (Chicago: Quadrangle Books, 1969), p. 42.

18. Thomas H. Patten, Jr., "Personnel Administration
and the Will to Manage," <u>Human Resources Management</u> 11
(Fall 1972): 7.

19. Ibid.

20. For a view of constructive conflict within an organizational context, see Joe Kelly, "Make Conflict Work
for You," <u>Harvard Business Review</u> 48 (July-August 1970):
103-13.

21. For a view of personnel as the manager of the organization's human capital, see Robert Wright, "Managing
Man as a Capital Asset," <u>Personnel Journal</u> 49 (April 1970):
290-98.

22. For an analysis of the relationship between scientific management and personnel policy, see V. Seymour Wilson, "The Relationship Between Scientific Management and
Personnel Policy in North American Administrative Systems,"
<u>Public Administration</u> 51 (Summer 1973): 193-205.

23. For a brief discussion of Herzberg's motivation-
hygiene concept, see Frederick Herzberg, "One More Time:
How Do You Motivate Employees?" <u>Harvard Business Review</u> 46
(January-February 1968).

24. "The Time Thieves," <u>Newsweek</u>, September 11, 1972,
p. 44.

25. David K. Shipler, "City Employees: On the Job
Vacations," New York <u>Times</u>, June 4, 1972, p. E5.

26. Letter of Karla J. Letsche, Washington <u>Post</u>, August 22, 1972, p. A19.

27. Marianne Means, "Nixon's Bureaucrats Are Not Too
Busy," <u>Times-Union</u> (Albany, N.Y.), November 1973.

28. U.S. Commission on Government Procurement, <u>Sum-
mary of the Report</u> (Washington, D.C.: U.S. Government
Printing Office, December 1972), p. 22.

29. Robert G. Wilmers and William F. Reilly, "Decay
in New York's Civil Service," <u>New Republic</u>, November 10,
1973, p. 19.

30. Manpower planning has only recently developed as
a discrete field of study. Some basic works: Edwin B.
Geisler, <u>Manpower Planning: An Emerging Staff Function</u>

(New York: American Management Association, 1967); Thomas
H. Patten, Jr., Manpower Planning and the Development of
Human Resources (New York: Wiley, 1971); Gareth Stainer,
Manpower Planning: The Management of Human Resources (London: Heinemann, 1971); Walter S. Wikstrom, Manpower Planning: Evolving Systems (New York: The Conference Board,
1971).

31. Report of a Special Task Force to the Secretary
of Health, Education, and Welfare, Work in America (Cambridge: The Massachusetts Institute of Technology Press,
1973), pp. xvii-xviii.

32. The American Telephone & Telegraph Company has
had one of the most successful and widely acclaimed programs. See Robert N. Ford, Motivation Through the Work Itself (New York: American Management Association, 1968).
For an update of the program five years later, see Robert
N. Ford, "Job Enrichment Lessons from At & T," Harvard
Business Review 51 (January-February 1973): 96-106. For
a review of the most successful industrial programs, see
HEW Task Force, Work in America, pp. 188-201.

33. The Bureau of the Budget required that, "Each department and agency will develop and maintain a position
management system designed to assure that the work is organized and assigned among positions in a manner which will
serve mission needs most effectively and economically. . . .
Position management includes the evaluation of the need
for positions and required skills and knowledge; and the
organization, grouping and assignment of duties and responsibilities among all positions. The position structure
should be designed to utilize the most effective work processes, equipment, procedures, methods and techniques."
Circular no. A-64 (revised), June 28, 1965.

34. Some examples of federal materials: U.S. Civil
Service Commission, Bureau of Intergovernmental Personnel
Programs, Job Analysis: Key to Better Management (Washington, D.C.: U.S. Government Printing Office, 1973); U.S.
Department of Labor, Manpower Administration, A Handbook
for Job Restructuring (Washington, D.C.: U.S. Government
Printing Office, 1970); Department of the Navy, Office of
Civilian Manpower Management, Resource Person's Guide for
Conducting Position Management Seminars (Washington, D.C.:
January 1972).

35. Fred K. Foulkes, Creating More Meaningful Work
(New York: American Management Association, 1969), p. 193.

36. An analysis of this problem is provided by M.
Scott Myers, "Overcoming Union Opposition to Job Enrichment," Harvard Business Review 49 (May-June 1971): 37-49.

37. Organizational development does not necessarily have to be traumatic. For the best single work on OD, see Wendell L. French and Cecil H. Bell, Jr., _Organization Development: Behavioral Science Interventions for Organization Improvement_ (Englewood Cliffs, N.J.: Prentice-Hall, 1973).

38. Donald R. Domm and James E. Stafford, "Personnel: Behind the Times," _Personnel Journal_ 49 (July 1970): 565.

39. It is already being predicted that organizational units of behavioral scientists "will function on a level above the Personnel Department." Jack H. Epstein and Robert H. Warren, "The Role of Behavioral Science in Organizations," in Herbert G. Hicks, ed., _Management, Organizations, and Human Resources: Selected Readings_ (New York: McGraw-Hill, 1972), p. 65.

5

PERSONNEL'S SYMBOLIC—BUT NOT FUTILE—GESTURES

Personnel operations still tend to live in the shadow of the old-style human relations approach to management that emphasized sympathetic attitudes on the part of managers and a healthy, happy catharsis on the part of the workers. Despite the plethora of research on organizational behavior and managerial phenomena in recent years, public personnel units are still blindly dishing out the human relations palliatives that have been so long discredited. The genesis of this attitude can be traced directly to the famous Hawthorne experiments that began in the 1920s.[1] Essentially these studies found that a manager's social skills were just as important as his technical expertise if he was to be an effective leader. The new-style manager would have to "maintain an equilibrium between the logic of efficiency and the nonlogic of worker sentiments."[2] The widespread influence of the Hawthorne studies was both a function of its inherent merit and, according to John M. Pfiffner, a function of the prestige of its sponsors--the Western Electric Company, the Harvard Business School, and the Rockefeller Foundation--in the eyes of the business community.[3] While the human relations in management approach was most influential during the late 1940s and 1950s, its critics consistently contended that it was little more than a gimmick, that there was sincere interest in the workers only to the extent that they could be manipulated for management's ends.[4] The goal was to adjust the worker--the same old interchangeable part of the scientific management movement--so that he would be content in the industrial situation, not to change the situation so that the worker would find contentment in his work.[5] The essential means of accomplishing this adjust-

ment was through satisfactory human associations. "Instead
of restoring man's pride in workmanship and allaying anomie,
human relations substituted a catharsis for the worker
rather than striking at the root of the problem, the nature
of the work itself."[6]

Some analysts maintain that the human relations movement has never really died out. Like the caterpillar that
turned into the butterfly, it simply matured into something
much more desirable. Human relations today is defined by
its supporters as the "application of the concepts and research methods of the behavioral sciences to the analysis
and understanding of organizational and administrative behavior."[7] Keith Davis argues that the human relations
movement has simply entered its mature period.[8] Thus, the
human relationists are able to expropriate all the appropriate behavioral advances as their own. Unfortunately,
most public personnel units, rather than accommodating
themselves to these new behavioral advances, have remained
with the initial phase and crude tools of the human relations movement.

Of course, personnel is not by any means entirely to
blame for this situation. When an employee problem arises
and management must take decisive action, what typically
happens? The personnel department with its bag of worn
palliatives is unleashed, and fast temporary relief from
managerial aggravation is achieved. But at what cost?
The problem is only temporarily pushed aside, and the personnel unit is maintained as a managerial jester capable
of briefly diverting attention but not of truly influencing
policy. According to Harry Levinson of the Harvard Business School, most industrial personnel efforts amount to
little more than "buying off" employees to keep them happy
by means of a thinly disguised paternalism; but such efforts are inherently incapable of resolving the myriad problems of the work situation. "In the absence of more effective problem-solving, the demand for palliation never
ceases."[9] Palliation, as the dictionary definition of the
word implies, can only mitigate or alleviate a situation;
it does not lead to actual changes.[10] This is a phenomenon
similar to an increase in what Frederick Herzberg would
call the "hygiene" factors of work--salary, working conditions, interpersonal relations, and so forth.[11] The demand for Herzberg's "hygiene" is similar to that of Levinson's "palliation"; it never ceases. "Hygiene acts like
heroin--it takes more and more to produce less and less
effect."[12] In this context it is the personnel department
that is called upon to play the morally corrupt role of the

narcotics pusher rather than the more socially redeeming role of the organizational physician.

While many of the larger private companies are conducting sincere experiments aimed at breaking away from the traditional personnel hypocrisies,[13] the public sector has continued to be dominated by the negative aspects of the public personnel mandate as they have been delineated in law and regulation. While there are exceptions, public personnel tends to suffer from what one of the leading textbooks on public administration has called "bureaucratic myopia: not keeping one's eye on the people for whom the system exists."[14] The real picture of American public personnel activities, according to Gerald E. Caiden, "is distorted by constant harping on the few showpieces in the public sector."[15]

What has caused personnel to be thrust into such a meager role and away from the substantive issues of human resources management? Part of the answer lies in the fact that the personnel unit has been significantly successful with its palliatives. But these successes are pyrrhic victories. An impressive-looking upward mobility, affirmative action, or career ladders program is of little consequence if its main purpose is simply to exist in response to and as a deflector of employee or outside pressures. With its host of palliatives and symbolic gestures, the personnel unit has become management's principal conveyer of the symbols of concern.

The manipulation of symbols and the dramaturgy of symbolic acts are essential elements in the maintenance of employee acquiescence. Whether such manipulations on the part of management are conscious or unconscious, they are invariably present. Frequently, symbolic acts are easily identifiable because of their obvious beau geste quality. They form an integral part of everyday manners and courtesies. When an organization's chief executive accidently meets a decidedly lower echelon employee in a crowded elevator and says, "How's your job coming along?" the executive is not using words to ask a question; the words are used simply to create an atmosphere of sociability. In this situation it would be out of place and both annoying and surprising to the executive if the employee answered the question at length instead of replying with a simple, "Fine, thank you." With this kind of social intercourse, words are used for their atmospheric quality rather than for their meaning. In consequence language ceases to be an instrument of communication and becomes a mode of action.[16] Such symbolic actions were the essence of the old

human relations approach to management. Personnel, when
it issues policies whose only effect is to waste paper,
when it consciously lies to its own as well as to the employees of the host organization, and when it boldly ex-
horts the workers to be more productive, is using words
as a substitute for action. Of course, such positive palliation is a highly viable administrative strategy used
at all managerial levels of society. Religious leaders
have been doing this effectively for centuries. Just as
the promise of an afterlife is a control on mortal behavior, the development of a symbolic upward mobility program serves as a damper on employee discontent. Similar
symbolic machinations are important devices for both control and motivation in any social system.

Since prehistory people have been effectively con-
trolled by their leaders by means of announced taboos and
mandated rituals. The associated symbolism portends either
terror or hope. American political leaders have evoked
terror with dire predictions about the "international communist conspiracy," and hope with a call to arms to fight
the "war on poverty." Similarly American business leaders
evoke terror by reminding us of the perils of bad breath,
dull teeth, and unsprayed bodily areas. These fears fade
when the various sprays, creams, gels, and pastes are pur-
chased and used. The public is assured that they too can
be "beautiful people" if they take the right vitamin supplements, drive the appropriate car, and drink the correct
diet cola. We are all subliminally, if not consciously,
aware of symbolism utilized in political rhetoric and business advertising. However, the vital role that symbolism
plays in policy making and managerial control in organizational and political situations is frequently unnoticed.

A political executive wishing to impose a sanction
upon a congressional committee that is holding up the funding of his programs might suggest that the committee is
not acting in "the national interest." The notion of "the
national interest," while vague, is a powerful symbol because it represents a commonly accepted good. Because
this good is so widely revered it has great legitimacy.[17]
Wise administrators will always "attempt to associate the
symbols of legitimacy with policies that they wish implemented."[18] By wrapping his program in a symbol of hefty
weight and using that symbol punitively against legislators
in opposition to his program, a political executive may
succeed in influencing those legislators. The success or
failure of such a calculated gambit depends upon a large
variety of interrelated factors. How susceptible to this

particular symbol were the legislators that he was trying to influence? Was the symbol of appropriate weight in comparison to the symbols of the opposition? While the political executive might have wished to use a heavier symbol, such a tactic might also backfire. One does not fight the opposition's symbol of "economy and efficiency" by calling them "communist dupes."

Conversely, symbols can be used to reward favorable action. After the political executive gets his desired appropriations, he might applaud the congressional committee members involved by publicly stating that they have shown "fiscal responsibility." Symbols may be analyzed and "presented on a continuum of punitiveness."[19] Such a continuum would have punitive symbols at one extreme, avoidance or threat symbols in the middle, and reward symbols at the other extreme. In order to apply the above discussion to a smaller scale, simply substitute "the good of the organization" or "the best interests of the city" for "the national interest." The difference between symbol usages in political and organizational contexts is merely one of vocabulary. Essentially the same considerations and tactics apply.

Experimenters have shown that there is a relation between culturally determined values and the perception of symbols. People will distort their perceptions of symbols according to the need for that which is symbolized.[20] Illustrative of this phenomenon is the national myopia concerning the social security program. America's first leap toward socialization was hailed as a triumph of capitalism. American political culture, while it may countenance socialistic measures, will not tolerate socialistic rhetoric. Thus, the Social Security Act was labeled an insurance system when "the bill in effect meant the same thing as if funds had been provided for by direct taxation."[21] American ideology favors the symbol "democracy" and abhors the symbol "socialism"; yet studies have shown that Americans are frequently operationally unsympathetic to democracy and sympathetic to socialism. A variety of surveys have shown that the majority of Americans responding "yes" when asked if they favored freedom of speech did not believe that communists should be allowed to speak publicly.[22]

Similarly, politicians and political executives tend to be rhetorically unsympathetic to spoils while at the same time being operationally in favor of abusive patronage privileges. In paying symbolic obeisance to the gods of civil service reform, the executive gains public acquiescence to pursue his personnel operations as he wishes.

This is quite in contrast to what would happen if an elected official publicly announced that he intended to use the civil service system to make political appointments. In having its elected leaders engage in widespread under- cover patronage in the name of a civil service merit sys- tem, American society achieves what Max J. Skidmore has termed a rhetorical reconciliation. Such a reconciliation is typically achieved when professed ideals conflict with accepted practices. Thus, accepted practices, such as il- legal patronage, are described in ideologically acceptable terms, such as merit system support. "The metamorphosis of the normal language shifts into a rhetorical reconcilia- tion between opposing practices and beliefs; a reconcilia- tion that serves to perpetuate the conflict by rationaliz- ing practices and delaying changes in ideology."[23]

Sociologist Erving Goffman has used the label "over- lays" to describe the practice of using a word or phrase to mean its opposite. "By judicious minor modification in timing and tone, in stress and gesture, overlays are possi- ble, that is, tacit meanings to be understood as contained in other meanings."[24] This is a common phenomenon in every- day life. Just think of the different meanings that a "thank you" can have. A person needing both hands to carry packages who has a door held open for him by some- one standing nearby would probably say "thank you." But if the individual standing idly nearby did nothing to as- sist the person with the packages as he struggled to open the door, a "thank you" from the struggler to the idler would have quite a different meaning because of the sarcasm implied by the situation. The same semantic overlays apply to the oft-professed verbal support that public officials give to merit system concepts. Thus, it is possible for them to abuse the merit system under their control while verbally supporting it, without any visible insincerity on their part. It is an occupational necessity for poli- ticians and personnelists alike to master the art of crea- tive ambiguity.[25]

Some people might be so crude as to label the practice of creative ambiguity as lying. But others would view it as the application of a time-tested administrative tech- nique merely applied to a lower political level. In her essay, "Lying in Politics," Hannah Arendt observes that "truthfulness has never been counted among the political virtues, and lies have always been regarded as justifiable tools in political dealings."[26] The pervasiveness of ly- ing by American political and administrative leaders is well known. Consequently, it is not unreasonable to find

microcosms of the larger political order--administrative
and political subsets--engaging in the same tactics.
Such tactics are both time honored and cross cultural. No
less a political adviser than Machiavelli himself gave
such advice in his most famous work, The Prince. Machiavelli urges the prospective leader (or administrator) "not
to keep faith when by so doing it would be against his interest."[27] Leaders ought to be great feigners and dissem-
blers because "men are so simple and so ready to obey present necessities, that one who deceives will always find
those who allow themselves to be deceived."[28]

Nowhere is primitive ritual or Machiavellian feigning
more apparent than in the periodic assumption of total responsibility by an organization's chief executive. One of
the advantages of delegating or relegating a problem to
the personnel department is the ease with which the cunning
manager can shift the blame for the situation if it sours
and complaints of inaction are brought to his attention.
Of course, modern executives are seldom so crude as to lay
the blame for a particular situation at the feet of the
personnel department, or any other department for that matter. The appropriate tactic would be to assume "full" responsibility for the situation. Paradoxically, in proclaim-
ing his assumption of full responsibility, the manager is
seemingly relieved of it. It is expected that the top management of any organizational unit will occasionally de-
clare its willingness, indeed eagerness, to take personal
responsbility for the actions and especially the mistakes
of subordinates. Whenever this ritual is enacted, all the
participants tend to experience "a warm glow of satisfaction and relief that responsibility has been assumed and
can be pinpointed. It once again conveys the message that
the incumbent is the leader, that he knows he is able to
cope, and that he should be followed."[29] In reality, however, this ritual proves to have no substance for it "em-
phatically does not mean that the chief executive will be
penalized for the mistakes of subordinates or that the
latter will not be penalized."[30] This is the tactic that
President Nixon employed when he first addressed the nation concerning the Watergate scandals in the spring of
1973. He boldly proclaimed that all the possibly illegal
actions of White House officials were his responsibility
and that he fully accepted that responsibility. While such
a gesture was not meaningless, it should have been recognized as nothing more than a symbolic gesture. Certainly
Nixon did not mean to imply that he should be punished for
the transgressions of his underlings. Government officials

of lesser rank are no less sophisticated with their manipulations of rituals and symbols.

Having an array of symbolic gestures at his command is a tremendous aid to an executive's dramaturgical performance.[31] When an executive is able to disarm the passions of aggrieved employees by ordering the personnel department to investigate the problem, he is fulfilling his dramaturgical role as a decisive and forceful leader of men, and the crisis is put off. Whether there was or was not any substance to the executive's directive is unimportant. A president of the United States acts in a similar manner when he establishes a national commission in a time of crisis. "Expected to respond to every public misfortune, the President has found that he can always respond on the plane of symbolic politics if not the plane of action."[32] The president, as any executive, must make a gesture to indicate his awareness of constituent distress. Whether that gesture has meaning or sincerity beyond itself is inconsequential for its immediate effect.[33] By the time a presidential commission makes its report or an ad hoc committee makes its recommendations to the organizational executive, six months to a year later, attention has been diverted to other issues, and the recommendations can be safely pigeonholed or curtailed. A commission or ad hoc committee fulfills its purpose when it serves "as a kind of tranquilizer to quiet public and congressional agitation."[34] One is reminded of Geoffrey Parsons' poem, "Royal Commission."

> If you're pestered by critics and hounded by faction
> To take some precipitate, positive action
> The proper procedure, to take my advice, is
> Appoint a Commission and stave off the crisis.[35]

Is it truly subterfuge or manipulation when employee groups, when calling for management to redress a real or imagined grievance, receive in return a symbolic gesture of some sort? James N. Rosenau has argued that "it is a gross misunderstanding of the functions of symbolic rewards to view their use as manipulation or deception."[36] After all, management does not have to approve of an employee demand in order to consider it. The admission that a demand is being considered reaffirms the right of employees to make such requests. Responding to the demand with a symbolic reward such as a phony upward mobility program not only acknowledges the appropriateness of the demand, but also establishes its legitimacy. Once the legitimacy of a demand is established, its eventual achievement, although it may be many years in coming, is practically preordained. However, if symbolic rewards were not provided in the meantime, employees would become dangerously alienated from the organization. Just as "it is the responsibility of leaders to provide symbolic rewards that build and sustain the citizenry's sense of political efficacy,"[37] it is the responsibility of management to provide the symbolic rewards that maintain the employees' sense of efficacy within the organization.

The personnel unit has a pivotal role in the creation and distribution of symbolic rewards. It is only personnel that can bestow the aegis of legitimacy upon a policy change. While line managers can only speak for their specific divisions, the personnel director speaks for the total organization. And personnel, because of all its previous associations with social concerns, symbolizes in itself a concern for the well-being of all employees. Consequently, its actions are almost viewed as those of a neutral third party using its good offices to resolve differences. Nowhere is this more true than in the public service, where personnel has the dual function of being at the same time a representative of management and the enforcer and interpreter of the civil service regulations. Because personnel, as a highly visible symbol in itself, is in an excellent posture to manipulate its own symbolic presentation, management has expected it to do just that. In the area of affirmative action programs, personnel departments in both the private and public sectors have been faced with situations rampant with symbolic overtones. With public pressure, federal legislation, and occasionally rioting employees all pressing for significant evidence of minority advancement, personnel has typically responded as the true son of management that it is. The never-ending search for the "best qualified" person continues apace, but with a new twist. Personnel managers now readily admit, in private, that they are just as likely to be looking for an "acceptable" black or an "acceptable" woman as for the "best possible" person for the job. Yet they are hardly in a position to publicize this fact. To admit that less-qualified blacks are hired and promoted would not only damage the self-image of innocent individuals, but would presumably create a considerable degree of animosity among other employees. So the fiction of being an "equal opportunity employer" remains. No less an establishment source than the Wall Street Journal has found that "the old American tradition of hiring the best man for the job is dying out, a victim of women's liberation, minority militancy and government regulation."[38]   An astute reader will, of course, recognize that this "old American tradition of hiring the best man" was as mythical then as "equal opportunity" is now.   Life--let alone administrative management--has never been, nor ever will be, that neat.

While government regulations have tended to generate advances for disadvantaged groups in private industry, advances in government organizations have frequently come as a result of confrontations. Affirmative action agitation has tended to be more severe in governmental organizations because elected and appointed officials are more susceptible to this kind of pressure than are their counterparts in the private sector. Government employees make their demands not only as employees but as citizens.   Thus, managers have to deal not just with aggrieved employees, but in the same instance with citizens petitioning their government.   Symbolic rewards and gestures more than anything else control the scope of conflict in such confrontation situations.   For that alone, symbols can be credited with holding the organization, as well as the larger polity, together.   While one party to a dispute may denounce as mere tokenism another party's response to their reasonable demands, such tokenism at least prevents the conflict from expanding.[39]   For example, the placing of an equal employment opportunity officer as a special assistant to the director of personnel, or even with rank equal to or greater than that of the personnel director, may be of little substantial import if the incumbent is given no staff support. But because the true intentions of the organization are in doubt, the establishment of a functionary at the highest hierarchal level is symbolically very important.[40]   By commanding attention such actions relieve pressure.   Nevertheless, public managers have not responded in any consistent fashion to confrontations with employee groups that demand, for example, an end to institutional racism within their organizations. When black employees of the Library of Congress staged a sit-in in the library's main reading room in order to dramatize their demands for higher pay, the director of personnel responded by offering to upgrade some of the job classifications in question.[41]   When the Department of Housing and Urban Development's employee organized "HUD Task Force Against Racial Discrimination" orchestrated demonstrations that led to Secretary George Romney's fleeing down 10 flights of stairs to an awaiting limousine with 300 demonstrators in pursuit,[42] the department responded by rescinding the initial disciplinary actions

taken against the employees[43] and implementing a variety
of upward mobility programs aimed at improving the status
of black employees.

Viewed systemically the primary function of a public
personnel unit "is not to guarantee the just treatment of
individuals but rather to symbolize the organization's intention to strive toward equitable behavior."[44] This is
not to say, however, that management consciously and deliberately assigns such a role to the personnel staff.
This is an inherent condition of personnel's uncomfortable
position as a form of administrative life that is neither
fully aligned with management or with the work force. The
best managers have always used this condition to their advantage. Executives who would admit great ignorance of the
behavioral analysis of organizations often operate in reality as if they were masters of the subject. Because of
what might be termed random learning, "it is possible for
organizational members to neither agree on nor know with
any certainty the value or purpose of a ceremonial, while
they continue to participate in and support such activities."[45] It has long been observed that successful managers of organizations are frequently unaware of the theoretical basis of actions that they perform artistically or
by instinct.[46]

It seems reasonable to hypothesize that symbols could
be used to greater advantage if they were employed with
some degree of calculation and awareness. The best politicians have always used symbols artfully and naturally;
administrators, if they wish their programs to be viable,
must learn to use them consciously and deliberately. If,
as many analysts maintain, symbolism is "at the heart of
the political process,"[47] then its manifestations would
apply at the micro level of the organizational unit as
well as the macro level of the greater polity. But since
there is no recognized body of administrative theory that
is "available to aid administrators in the development of
a consistent and professional response to . . . conflict
and confrontation,"[48] a further analysis of the viability
of symbolic responses in conflict situations would be a
logical first step toward the development of a practical
theory. Only with the systemic evaluation and empirical
testing of the propositions concerning the myriad facets
of political symbolism will its study "be moved from the
realm of speculation and argument and elevated to the
status of rigorous scientific inquiry."[49]

NOTES

1. For the definitive account of the Hawthorne experiments, see F. J. Roethlisberger and William J. Dickson, Management and the Worker (Cambridge, Mass.: Harvard University Press, 1939).

2. Daniel A. Wren, The Evolution of Management Thought (New York: Ronald Press, 1972), p. 299.

3. John M. Pfiffner and Marshall Fels, The Supervision of Personnel: Human Relations in the Management of Men, 3d ed. (Englewood Cliffs, N.J.: Prentice-Hall, 1964), pp. 20-21; John M. Pfiffner and Frank P. Sherwood, Administrative Organization (Englewood Cliffs, N.J.: Prentice-Hall, 1960), pp. 101-02.

4. Henry A. Landsberger, Hawthorne Revisited (Ithaca, N.Y.: Cornell University Press, 1958), pp. 29-30. This book is a critique of the wake of the Hawthorne experiments.

5. Daniel Bell labeled this approach that equated contented with productive workers as "cow sociology," presumably after the Carnation Milk cows that gave more milk because they were contented. Work and Its Discontents: The Cult of Efficiency in America (Boston: Beacon Press, 1956), p. 25.

6. Wren, The Evolution of Management Thought, pp. 372-73.

7. David G. Moore, "Human Relations in Organization," in Sidney Mailick and Edward H. Van Ness, eds., Concepts and Issues in Administrative Behavior (Englewood Cliffs, N.J.: Prentice-Hall, 1962), p. 187.

8. Keith Davis, Human Behavior at Work: Human Relations and Organizational Behavior, 4th ed. (New York: McGraw-Hill, 1972), p. 11.

9. Harry Levinson, The Exceptional Executive: A Psychological Conception (Cambridge, Mass.: Harvard University Press, 1968), p. 225.

10. For a discussion of why personnel is not more of a change agent, see Chapter 4.

11. For the original account of Herzberg's motivation-hygiene theory, see Frederick Herzberg, Bernard Mausner, and Barbara B. Snyderman, The Motivation to Work (New York: Wiley, 1959).

12. Frederick Herzberg, Work and the Nature of Man (Cleveland: World Publishing Company, 1966), p. 170.

13. Some of the best accounts of successful experiments are Robert N. Ford, Motivation Through the Work Itself (New York: American Management Association, 1969); John R. Maher, ed., New Perspectives in Job Enrichment

(New York: Van Nostrand Reinhold Co., 1971); M. Scott
Myers, Every Employee a Manager (New York: McGraw-Hill,
1970); W. J. Paul and K. B. Robertson, Job Enrichment and
Employee Motivation (London: Gower Press, 1970); Peter P.
Schoderbek and William E. Reif, Job Enlargement: Key to
Improved Performance (Ann Arbor: Bureau of Industrial Re-
lations, University of Michigan, 1969).

14.   Marshall E. Dimock and Gladys O. Dimock, Public
Administration, 4th ed. (New York: Holt, Rinehart and
Winston, 1969), p. 218. The Dimocks' statement is reminiscent of Wallace Sayre's title for his analysis of public
personnel operations: "The Triumph of Techniques over
Purpose," Public Administration Review, vol. 8 (Spring
1948).

15.   Gerald E. Caiden, The Dynamics of Public Administration: Guidelines to Current Transformations in Theory
and Practice (New York: Holt, Rinehart and Winston, 1971),
p. 211.

16.   This phenomenon is called "phatic communion."
Hugh D. Duncan, Communication and Social Order (New York:
Bedminster Press, 1962), p. 36. Duncan's source for his
discussion of phatic communion is Bronislaw Malinowski,
"The Problem of Meaning in Primitive Languages," in C. K.
Ogden and I. A. Richards, eds., The Meaning of Meaning: A
Study of the Influence of Language upon Thought and of the
Science of Symbolism (New York: Harcourt, Brace, 1945),
p. 316.

17.   The ideal of legitimacy is used in a psychological
as opposed to a moral sense. "Psychologically an action
is legitimate when it is popularly so accepted." David
Easton, The Political System: An Inquiry into the State
of Political Science, 2d ed. (New York: Knopf, 1971), p.
159n.

18.   Richard M. Merelman, "Learning and Legitimacy,"
American Political Science Review 60 (1966): 553.

19.   Ibid., p. 555.

20.   James C. Davis, Human Nature in Politics: The
Dynamics of Political Behavior (New York: Wiley, 1963),
p. 121.

21.   Thurman W. Arnold, The Symbols of Government
(New Haven, Conn.: Yale University Press, 1935), p. 121.

22.   Fred I. Greenstein, The American Party System and
the American People (Englewood Cliffs, N.J.: Prentice-Hall,
1963), pp. 7-9.

23.   Max J. Skidmore, Medicare and the American Rhetoric of Reconciliation (University: University of Alabama
Press, 1970), p. 19.

24. Erving Goffman, Relations in Public: Microstudies of the Public Order (New York: Harper Colophon Books, 1972), p. 167.

25. For a discussion of the value of ambiguous language, see Donald W. Hastings and Glenn M. Vernon, "Ambiguous Language as a Strategy for Individual Action," Journal of Applied Behavioral Science 7 (May-June 1971): 371-75.

26. Hannah Arendt, Crises of the Republic (New York: Harcourt, Brace, Jovanovich, 1972), p. 4.

27. Niccolo Machiavelli, The Prince and The Discourses (New York: Modern Library, 1950), p. 64.

28. Ibid., pp. 64-65. For modern applications of Machiavelli's techniques, see Richard P. Calhoon, "Niccolo Machiavelli and the Twentieth Century Administrator," Academy of Management Journal 12 (June 1969): 205-12; Anthony Jay, Management and Machiavelli: An Inquiry into the Politics of Corporate Life (New York: Holt, Rinehart and Winston, 1967).

29. Murray Edelman, The Symbolic Uses of Politics (Urbana: University of Illinois Press, 1967), p. 79.

30. Ibid.

31. For a definitional discussion of dramaturgy, see Victor A. Thompson, Modern Organization (New York: Knopf, 1969), ch. 7, pp. 138-51.

32. Martha Derthick, "On Commissionship-Presidential Variety," Public Policy 19 (Fall 1971): 630.

33. Discussions of this can be found in Frank Popper, The President's Commissions (New York: Twentieth Century Fund, 1970), p. 9; and Robert Reinhold, "Results Termed Mixed for Study Panels," New York Times, March 28, 1971, p. 48.

34. Harold Seidman, Politics, Position, & Power: The Dynamics of Federal Organization (New York: Oxford University Press, 1970), p. 23. This is a time-honored presidential gambit. Herbert Hoover even admits to it in his memoirs. See Herbert C. Hoover, The Memoirs of Herbert Hoover: The Cabinet and the Presidency, 1920-1933 (New York: Macmillan, 1952), p. 281.

35. For the complete poem, see Punch, August 24, 1955, or Claude E. Hawley and Ruth G. Weintraub, eds., Administrative Questions and Political Answers (Princeton, N.J.: D. Van Nostrand, 1966), p. 204.

36. James N. Rosenau, "Public Protest, Political Leadership and Diplomatic Strategy," Orbis 14 (Fall 1970): 568.

37. Ibid., p. 569.

38. Ralph E. Winter, "All Applying Are Equal, But Some Are More So at Many Companies," _Wall Street Journal_, June 6, 1973, p. 1.

39. Roger W. Cobb and Charles D. Elder, _Participation in American Politics: The Dynamics of Agenda-Building_ (Boston: Allyn and Bacon, Inc., 1972), p. 127.

40. Edelman, _The Symbolic Uses of Politics_, p. 63.

41. For accounts of this incident, see the Washington _Post_, June 26, 1971; _Federal Times_, July 14, 1971.

42. New York _Times_, October 11, 1970, p. 82; October 15, 1970, p. 43.

43. Washington _Star_, November 24, 1971.

44. Harrison M. Trice, James Belasco, and Joseph A. Allutto, "The Role of Ceremonials in Organizational Behavior," _Industrial and Labor Relations Review_ 23 (October 1969): 50.

45. Ibid., p. 42.

46. This phenomenon has frequently been demonstrated by examinations of the formal/informal dichotomy existing in all organizations. See Chester I. Barnard, _The Functions of the Executive_, 30th anniversary ed. (Cambridge, Mass.: Harvard University Press, 1968), pp. 120-22.

47. Roger W. Cobb and Charles D. Elder, "The Political Uses of Symbolism," _American Politics Quarterly_ 1 (July 1973): 305.

48. Arnold J. Auerbach, "Confrontation and Administrative Response," _Public Administration Review_ 29 (November-December 1969): 640.

49. Cobb and Elder, "The Political Uses of Symbolism," p. 335.

6

**PERSONNEL—
THE ORGANIZATIONAL
UNDERACHIEVER**

The differences between public personnel administration and public personnel management are more than semantic. The former is mainly concerned with the technical aspects of maintaining a full complement of employees within an organization, while the latter concerns itself with the larger problems of the viability of an organization's human resources. Personnel management tends to go by default in most public agencies because the traditional administrative role of the personnel office creates an artificial and frequently self-imposed boundary on the scope of activities. Consequently, public personnel operations have tended to deal with the more superficial aspects of the management process rather than placing itself in the vanguard of organizational renewal. As a result, important issues central to a viable management program and integrally part of the personnel function are left unexplored. It is as if there is a conspiracy of silence concerning certain unmentionable problems, such as the corruption and incompetence of certain employees.

This is a phenomenon similar to that described by Peter Bachrach and Morton Baratz in their article concerning decisions and nondecisions.[1] They found that powerful interests within the community were able to limit the scope of political decision making by the mere force of their presence. Elected as well as appointed public executives, by giving conscious or unconscious deference to these power forces, restricted their own policy options. Similarly, public personnel units, because of the inferior organizational positions that they typically occupy, have their scope of policy initiation severely limited. Personnel's position is inherently inferior to that of other staff functions because most executives, being unable to have complete control of personnel's operations, will not trust it--and with good reason. One would be naturally disinclined to confer important responsibilities upon a staff whose loyalty lies at least in part with another agency--the civil service commission. Fully aware of its position as an organizational stepchild, personnel tends to use its decisional discretion to make "safe" decisions that do not adversely affect any of the vital interests of the power forces aligned against the personnel establishment. Thus, a personnel unit seeking to enhance its organizational reputation as a "can do" operation is likely to unveil a new program for performance reporting, but is unlikely to launch a large-scale effort to weed out marginal and incompetent employees.

Employee rating programs, as commonly administered, are just one example of the futility of many of personnel's traditional functions. Performance reports tend to be harmless to all concerned. Since virtually everyone falls into the satisfactory category,[2] the ratings mainly serve to fulfill the personnel department's penchant for impressive-looking rating forms, orderly files, and "significant" work. Many jurisdictions have performance rating systems required by legislation or operating mandate.[3] Frequently, these laws provide that annual ratings should be a pertinent factor in determining salary increases, promotions, and--in the event of reductions in force--the order of layoffs.[4] However, because the norm is a satisfactory rating, the ratings seldom serve any real purpose. For example, the city of Philadelphia has extremely formal and elaborate performance rating procedures; but a survey of Philadelphia's managerial employees found that over 60 percent of them felt that the performance rating procedures were either irrelevant, discredited, or unfair.[5]

While in the past ratings were ineffective because of the lethargy of top management and informal organizational norms, their newly weakened condition is caused by the comparatively recent strength of employee organizations. Whether they be professional associations, fraternal orders of police, or plain old-fashioned unions, such groups will not meekly tolerate a hard-nosed management effort at performance ratings. In many jurisdictions their power base, their clout, is such that a personnel director has better sense than to tangle with them even over such a basic issue as competence on the job. But what good is a rating system if it cannot be used as a discriminator for awarding promotions or merit pay increases? Municipal employee unions are so strong in New York City, for example, that agency officials almost unanimously admitted to being "prevented . . . from effectively using disciplinary measures to weed out unfit employees or to stimulate others to better performance."[6]

The reprehensible situation that commonly prevails with performance reporting illustrates what Bachrach and Baratz have called nondecision making--"the practice of limiting the scope of actual decision-making to 'safe' issues by manipulating the dominant community values, myths, and political institutions and procedures."[7] There is an air of safeness and dullness about the practice of public personnel administration largely because it fears to go beyond the artificial boundaries created by the power forces in its environment. Rather than act upon its own initiatives and take an expansive view of its responsibilities, personnel units tend to stifle their imaginations and take the cues for their behavior from a variety of external sources. Instead of questioning the values established for it by the dominant members of the administrative community and the unions, it limply accepts a mandate for underachievement. Raymond D. Horton has provided a perfect example of this phenomenon in his analysis of municipal labor relations in New York City. In 1971 when a periodic financial crisis prompted city officials to publicly proclaim their intention to press hard during collective bargaining with uniformed employees for changes in the work rules that would enhance productivity, "the incongruity of public officials having even to bargain over changes they were legally free to implement went unnoticed."[8] The leadership of the employee organizations was so successful at manipulating community values and institutions that top city management had substantially yielded their discretional prerogatives over work rules even before the start of negotiations.

Frequently the personnel unit walks blindly amid a sea of malfeasance and corruption, protected from confronting reality by obfuscating procedures and a lacking sense of mission. For proof one need only examine the enduring problem of bribery. Viewed systemically bribery is an important element in the American political system. It supplements the salaries of various public officials. Many policemen and building inspectors, for example, would be unable to maintain their present standard of living if it were not for such informal salary increments. Additionally, such income supplement programs forestall the need for politically unpopular precipitous tax hikes that would bring the legal wages of such officers up to reasonable levels. Systematic bribery allows businessmen, dependent upon the discretionary powers of public officials for their livelihood, to stabilize the relationships essential for the smooth functioning of their businesses. Its occasional exposure by a troublesome press serves to foster the political alienation of the electorate, which in turn encourages cynicism and reduces support for the democratic processes of government. While it is possible to quibble over the particulars of any given instance or noninstance of bribery, its pervasiveness in American government is generally not contested except by the most naive or the most corrupt. Official recognition of this popularly recognized problem was provided by the National Advisory Commission on Criminal Justice when it reported that governmental corruption "stands as a serious impediment to the task of reducing criminality in America."[9] A preliminary report of the commission concluded that as long as official corruption flourished, "the war against crime will be perceived by many as a war of the powerful against the powerless; 'law and order' will be a hypocritical rallying cry, and 'equal justice under the law' will be an empty phrase."[10] In 1971 the attorney general of the United States reported that over 170 state and local public officials and ex-officials had been indicted or convicted during the past two years as part of the Justice Department's drive against organized crime and corruption.[11] Of course, such numbers represent only the tip of the proverbial iceberg.

While there are isolated pockets of rectitude, just as there are instances of abject venality, most communities come to tolerate the systematic corruption of their officials through one of three different patterns of toleration: a nonenforcement policy, community indifference, or community encouragement.[12]

Nonenforcement policies exist for an otherwise honest public servant when officials above him in the organizational hierarchy are corrupt. An honest subordinate saddled with a nonenforcement policy has a variety of options. He can become corrupt himself, resign his position, or remain in the system as a force for good. Another logical alternative, going to the police or the courts, is frequently not viable. For obvious reasons police departments tend to be the bellwethers of systemic programs of corruption. The only thing surprising about this is the feigned shock political leaders display when confronted with appropriate evidence. The most publicized police exposés of recent years were the Knapp Commission hearings in New York

City.[13] Yet the hearings turned up nothing that had not been well documented about big city police operations since the Wickersham Commission in the early 1930s.[14] What Sayre and Kaufman have said about New York City police in their well-known book, Governing New York City, is equally true, except for isolated areas, for the rest of the nation. A police commissioner or chief must accept that "corruption is endemic to his organization, and that he is fortunate if he can prevent it from reaching epidemic proportions."[15]

As a rule of thumb, the local courts with their attendant judicial machinery tend to follow the degree of corruption exhibited by the police.[16] Judicial corruption has even been proven quantifiably, if not specifically, by the New York State Joint Legislative Committee on Crime. The committee found that over a ten-year period (1960-69), state supreme court judges dismissed 11.5 percent of indictments against all defendants; but they dismissed 44.7 percent of indictments against organized crime figures.[17] In cases where organized crime members were actually convicted, 46 percent of them were merely given suspended sentences or fines.[18] While it is more comforting to dwell upon just justices and honest police, thoughtful citizens do not necessarily have to be total cynics in order to support Daniel Moynihan's contention that "corruption by organized crime is a normal condition of American local government and politics."[19]

Because he is frequently caught between the nonenforcement policy of administrative superiors and the perceived hostile attitudes on the part of the criminal justice system, an "honest" public servant frequently has no practical choice but to accommodate himself to this situation. Of course, there are a variety of ways he could "go public" with what he knows; but it takes an exceptional individual to bear the ensuing hostility and social ostracism of his colleagues. Ralph Nader has urged congressional legislation to protect employees who speak out against governmental activities that are harmful to the public welfare.[20] Nader and his supporters have written widely about the desirability of fostering a "whistleblowing" ethic in government.[21] They have even established a Clearinghouse for Professional Responsibility as part of the larger Public Interest Research Group. The clearinghouse will serve both to encourage disclosures and to protect employees against employer retaliation.[22] While there have been some successes in this area, the total impact of this new employee ethic has been marginal to date.

The second manner in which a community tolerates corruption is through indifference; but indifference in this case amounts to consent. Any community unwilling to devote the necessary resources to weed out corrupting influences tacitly deserves the conditions that it inadvertently supports.

Finally, the corruption of the public service is frequently encouraged and supported by many of the "leading" citizens of the community. As Robert C. Wood observed almost two decades ago, "public and private ethics are inseparably intertwined."[23] A society cannot reasonably maintain moral standards for its public officials that grossly differ from those of the remainder of the community. While it is not illegal for a businessman to tip a truck driver to insure that a valuable shipment arrives on time, it is quite illegal to tip a municipal construction inspector to insure that he arrives at the construction site at an agreed-upon time. If a plumbing inspector arrives two hours later than his appointment, this could cost the contractor thousands of dollars in unnecessary payroll, since the brickmasons, carpenters, and plasterers, for example, cannot begin their work until the plumbing has been inspected. It is simply good business sense for the contractor to tip the plumbing inspector $20 to show up on time rather than risk having a variety of skilled workers idle for several expensive hours. But, once started, this tipping of government officials frequently has no end. Building plans must be expedited through city architectural reviewers. Police must allow construction equipment to be illegally parked on side streets. "Construction men insist that the bribes merely avoid harassment by inspectors, policemen and others whose power to delay work can cost thousands of dollars a day."[24] It is estimated that about 5 percent of the cost of construction in New York goes for bribes of public officials.[25] During a periodic crackdown on corruption among municipal building inspectors, the president of the Allied Building Inspectors Union noted that bribery has persisted over the years. "This is another generation of inspectors that are being corrupted--it's not the men, they don't have criminal backgrounds. It's the system."[26] The system is quite generous. Some inspectors have been able to triple their annual salaries through it!

Where is the personnel department when all this is going on? No doubt it is tending to its position classifications and developing new performance reporting forms. Are personnelists so naive that they do not know what is going on? Probably not. Personnel people are no different from others in the community. It is fair to presume that they are as knowledgeable of corrupt practices as are other politically aware individuals. Their inaction is largely due to their inferior organizational position and lack of imagination, rather than to ignorance of what is going on. Besides, personnelists play only a small role in the adverse action proceedings that are necessary to remove a malfeasant employee. Because evidence must be assembled and care must be taken for constitutional and procedural safeguards, removal initiatives must generally come from the line manager and/or the legal division. If they are unwilling or unable to take such action, personnel has little real choice but to acquiesce.

Yet there is much that a creative personnel department could do to remedy the severity of corruption. If the problem is viewed systemically, the solution lies in providing systemic safeguards. For example, it has frequently been demonstrated that construction inspectors have a gift for bribery. By examining the inspection system, the personnel department can intervene at specific points to make successful bribery much less likely. While personnel has no influence over the building industry, it has a considerable amount of generally unused discretion over employee populations--construction inspectors included. Since it would be of only temporary benefit to change the inspectors if the system remained static, the personnel department can change the nature of the inspectors to great effect by altering both the character of the position and the recruiting base for new inspectors. Instead of using former construction trade personnel as inspectors, only junior college or liberal arts graduates could be recruited. This group is plentiful, can be had relatively cheaply, and should be amenable to an intensive training program in inspection skills. The next step is to restructure the inspector's job so that it is not a dead-end position but the beginning rung on a career ladder eventually leading to management positions, and see that the duties and responsibilities are expanded to include a variety of activities appropriate to a professional position.

While professional-style employees may be no more honest than others, it is at least reasonable to hypothesize that their attitudes and incentives would lead them to behave differently from those who have been proven unable to deal with temptation. What is significant here is not this specific example dealing with construction inspectors, but the suggestion of a methodology for weeding out recur-

99

rent patterns of corruption. While it is possible that experts in construction or inspection programs could find fault with the example, the methodology would, nevertheless, remain valid for inspector positions as well as for other job titles.

In addition to alterations in the recruiting base and the redesign of positions, personnel could more aggressively use the skills at which it typically excels in most large jurisdictions. There is substantial evidence that marginal, dishonest, and troublesome employees can be identified through a more sophisticated approach to examining procedures, statistical studies, and probationary periods. For example, a New York City-Rand Institute study of 2,000 New York policemen who joined the department in 1957 found that those who ended up with poor records in subsequent years could have been easily identified during their nine-month probationary period if only they had been subjected to better testing methods. Of the men who had at least one unsatisfactory incident during their probationary periods, "fully 35 percent were convicted of corruption or some other serious infraction."[27] This rate was 50 percent higher than for those men without unsatisfactory ratings during this period. Meanwhile, the New York City Police Department, confident of its sense of priorities, had the time to seek out and dismiss a patrolman for living with a woman to whom he was not legally wed, on the grounds that such behavior "brought adverse criticism on the department."[28]

While a probationary period is in theory an on-the-job extension of the total civil service examining process, in practice employees in almost all jurisdictions are automatically retained unless they do something grossly untoward. Such customs are not easily altered. When the deputy mayor of New York suggested new procedures under which probationary employees would be automatically fired unless supervisors specifically recommended otherwise, the various municipal employee unions responded with threats of court challenges.[29]

Unfortunately, the political and organizational environment of the personnel unit tends to severely limit its methodological imagination. With unions pulling in one direction, management in another, and conscience perhaps dictating a third, it is little wonder that personnel acts a bit paranoid and withdrawn. Not only need personnel be wary of threatening forces in its immediate environs, but it never really knows when forces in its penumbra will make their presence known. For example, how far could major revisions in the inspection system get before the politically well-connected construction industry used their substantial clout to stop any such program? As Lincoln Steffens observed early in this century, the respectable business leaders of the community are frequently as dependent upon the corruption of government as corrupt government officials are dependent upon them.

A reasonable person could accept the preceding discussion as valid and still rebut the basic contention that the personnel agency is in any way negligent. After all, the corruption of public office is a systemic problem totally integrated with the local political culture and ultimately dependent upon executive compliance. To blame personnel for this state of affairs would be akin to blaming a child for being born into a family of thieves. But if personnel does not acknowledge a large measure of responsibility for these clearly "personnel" problems, it loses by default any claim that it may have had to professional status. Because the personnel function has been perceived by management to be that of system maintenance rather than system improvement, personnel staffs have tended to accommodate themselves to housekeeping or clerical functions. Consequently, American civil service system administrators have well-earned reputations for excelling with record-keeping systems, position classification programs, and all the marginally consequential aspects of personnel management.

The organizational impotence of typical public personnel offices must be kept in perspective. Their counterparts in the private sector tend to fair no better, albeit for different reasons. The well-known organizational analyst Warren G. Bennis has written that on the basis of his "experience with government and even more with industry, it seems that personnel men become more or less the servants of power rather than being active, aggressive and assertive in a strong leadership way."[30] The bad-mouthing of personnel in the private sector is equal to the denigration of personnel by public executives; to a significant degree it becomes a self-fulfilling prophecy. Individuals with large talents and ambitions to match are unlikely to enter or remain in an organizational unit that will reflect poorly upon their professional standing. Remaining in personnel are those with lesser abilities, lesser ambitions, and lesser reputations. Chris Argyris, one of the foremost authorities on organizational development, admits that he will only rarely accept a consulting invitation from a personnel officer. Simply, generally, and generously put, "personnel men aren't up-to-date in the field of behavioral sciences."[31]

Public personnel operatives, having not been allowed to cope with many of the more pertinent issues of public employment, have frequently grown unable to do so. In consequence, the underlying premises of their limited mandate are accepted and the pains of underachievement are avoided by the simple expedient of seeking to achieve so little.

NOTES

1. Peter Bachrach and Morton S. Barartz, "Decisions and Nondecisions: An Analytical Framework," American Political Science Review 57 (December 1963): 632-42.

2. This was the finding of a major study of the federal performance rating program. Mary S. Schinagl, History of Efficiency Ratings in the Federal Government (New York: Bookman Associates, 1966), p. 87.

3. The federal rating system was established by the Performance Rating Act of 1950, Public Law 81-873.

4. These provisions are all included in the rating system of the city of Philadelphia. They were mandated by the City Charter. See Philadelphia Home Rule Charter, Section 7-401(n).

5. Jay M. Shafritz, The Municipal Middle Management System in Philadelphia (Ph.D. dissertation, Temple University, 1971), p. 185. Fitness ratings take on comical proportions in the military where an officer merely rated "excellent," instead of "outstanding" or "exceptional" is considered to be mediocre. For a discussion of this, see the chapter entitled, "The Best Officer I Have Ever Seen," in Stuart H. Loory, Defeated: Inside America's Military Machine (New York: Random House, 1973).

6. Raymond D. Horton, Municipal Labor Relations in New York City: Lessons of the Lindsay-Wagner Years (New York: Praeger, 1973), p. 115.

7. Bachrach and Baratz, "Decisions and Nondecisions: An Analytical Framework," p. 632.

8. Horton, Municipal Labor Relations in New York City, p. 107. In the midst of all the publicity about obtaining more productivity from the uniformed services, the New York Times reported that "some sanitation policemen have charged they've been under pressure to sell tickets to a dinner for Mayor Lindsay." A "City Hall regular" is quoted as saying, "cutting out that kind of stuff could mean a big jump in

102

productivity." New York Times, November 21, 1971, p. E7.
A week later a deputy sanitation commissioner resigned
amid accusations that his men were being "strongarmed" into
buying tickets for the mayor's fund-raising dinner. New
York Times, November 18, 1971, p. 1.

9. New York Times, August 19, 1973, p. 41.

10. Ibid. It is ironic that the commission was formed
at the suggestion of former Attorney General Mitchell, who
was subsequently indicted on charges relating to corruption.

11. New York Times, October 21, 1971, p. 4. For a popular documentation of organized crime's pervasive influence
with political leaders, see Clark R. Mollenhoff, Strike
Force: Organized Crime and the Government (Englewood
Cliffs, N.J.: Prentice-Hall, 1972).

12. This delineation was established in regard to
police corruption by Donald R. Cressey, Theft of the Nation: The Structure and Operations of Organized Crime in
America (New York: Harper Colophon Books, 1969), pp. 275-81.

13. For brief accounts of the Knapp Commission Hearings, see Newsweek, November 1, 1971; January 3, 1972.

14. President Hoover appointed George W. Wickersham,
the former attorney general under President Taft, to chair
a commission that would examine American law enforcement
machinery. The most pertinent formal report to come out
of this was the United States National Commission on Law
Observance and Enforcement, Report on Lawlessness in Law
Enforcement (Washington, D.C.: U.S. Government Printing
Office, 1931). V. O. Key, Jr.'s classic 1935 article on
police graft could seemingly have been written by a Knapp
Commission staffer; see V. O. Key, Jr., "Police Graft,"
American Journal of Sociology 40 (March 1935): 624-36.

15. Wallace S. Sayre and Herbert Kaufman, Governing
New York City: Politics in the Metropolis (New York: W.
W. Norton, 1965), p. 289.

16. For a nationwide account of judicial corruption,
see Charles R. Ashman, The Finest Judges Money Can Buy
(Los Angeles: Nash Publishing Corp., 1973).

17. Report of the New York State Joint Legislative
Committee on Crime, Its Causes, Control and Effect on Society, Legislative Document no. 26 (Albany, September 1,
1971), p. 84.

18. Ibid., p. 85.

19. Daniel P. Moynihan, "The Private Government of
Organized Crime," Reporter 25 (July 6, 1961): 14. This is
further supported by the President's Commission on Law Enforcement and Administration of Justice, Task Force Report:
Organized Crime (Washington, D.C.: U.S. Government Printing Office, 1967).

20. New York *Times*, January 15, 1971, p. 43.

21. Two examples of this genre: Ralph Nader, Peter J. Petkas, and Kate Blackwell, eds., Whistle Blowing: The Report of the Conference on Professional Responsibility (New York: Grossman, 1972); Charles Peters and Taylor Branch, eds., Whistle Blowing: Dissent in the Public Interest (New York: Praeger, 1972).

22. New York *Times*, January 27, 1971, p. 32.

23. Robert C. Wood, "Ethics in Government as a Problem in Executive Management," Public Administration Review 15 (Winter 1955).

24. David K. Shipler, "Bribery: For Builders It's a $25-Million Routine," New York *Times*, July 2, 1972, p. E10.

25. Harlow Unger, "Bribes Expedite All New York Building," Washington *Post*, August 27, 1972, p. F1.

26. David K. Slipler, "Inspectors' Union Refuses Support for Graft Study," New York *Times*, July 30, 1972, p. 1.

27. "How to Prune the Police," Newsweek, May 22, 1972.

28. Playboy, November 1968, p. 70.

29. New York *Times*, November 16, 1972, p. 1.

30. Warren G. Bennis, "Human Society in the Seventies," in Warren G. Bennis et al., Personnel Dialogue for the Seventies (Chicago: Public Personnel Association, Personnel Report no. 712, 1971), p. 5.

31. Harold M. F. Rush, "Behavioral Scientist at Large . . . A Candid Conversation with Chris Argyris," in Wendell L. French and Don Hellriegel, eds., Personnel Management and Organization Development: Fields in Transition (Boston: Houghton Mifflin Co., 1971), p. 25. This article originally appeared in Conference Board Record 4 (May 1967): 23-28.

7

THE NETHERWORLD
OF PUBLIC
PERSONNEL
MANAGEMENT

Outwardly the practice of public personnel administration seems to operate in a dull, plodding manner. While the merit system ebbs and flows, so little research is done in this area that few academics would take quick notice if this tide went out one day and never returned. Serious overviews of the public personnel function invariably bemoan the fact that the field generates so little research. As this limited amount of scholarly effort finds that public personnel administration is covered by a "deadly haze of boredom,"[1] guarded by a "veil of ennui,"[2] or living "in the doldrums";[3] new research initiatives are effectively discouraged. The lack of academic interest in the field is illustrated by a survey of the subfield choices of over 7,265 members of the American Political Science Association. In a rank order list of 27 areas of specialization, public personnel administration came out in last place.[4] The intellectual sterility of the field is formally attested to in appropriate journals and textbooks. One writer has observed that the authors of the standard works in this area "seem to have contracted some malignant Midas touch which enables them to turn even cosmic matters into utter banalities."[5] Hopefully, this is not contagious. In 1961 the most reputable historian of the United States civil service, Paul P. Van Riper, wrote that he could find "little in print concerning the American civil service and American public personnel administration which can be termed either exciting or intellectually stimulating in any fundamental sort of way."[6] His statement remains equally valid today. The professional literature in the field is limited in more ways than in quantity. Upon examining the standard public personnel texts,[7] one is re-

minded of a British reviewer's remark about an earlier
academic work of Henry Kissinger's: "I don't know if Mr.
Kissinger is a great writer, but anyone finishing his book
is a great reader."[8]

In spite of its protective shield of dullness, the
public personnel world offers a considerable amount of ex-
citement and dynamism that goes all but unobserved by the
outsider--be he scholar, journalist, or citizen. Almost
hidden from the public policy analysts is a public personnel netherworld deeply reflective of the turbulence and
conflicts of the greater society. It is a world largely
inhabited by well-meaning and sincere individuals--the
whole gamut of personnel operaties--who are forced by the
circumstances of their lives to engage in prostitution,
illegal patronage, and perversion. Prostitution in this
context refers to the performance of acts that are sometimes illegal as well as being morally and ethically repug-
nant--and doing so for the sake of money--that is, to keep
one's job. Illegal patronage refers to the practice of
requiring political clearances for normally established
merit system positions. Perversion refers to the administration of the civil service regulations so that portions
of them are relegated to being fictions operable only in
a fantasy world.

These are serious allegations likely to arouse the
wrath of many of the participants in this netherworld. No-
body wants to be charged with prostitution or perversion.
However, these are not the isolated allegations of a single writer but reflect the totality of the views of many
of the netherworld inhabitants. Unfortunately, there has
been little direct research in this area. It is always
immensely difficult to gather data on activities that are
of doubtful propriety or obvious illegality.[9] The incon-
clusive data available on the extent of organized crime
is a ready example. A general study on administration
circumvention concluded that the slight amount of literature on this subject was "due to the fact that deviation
is usually hidden beyond recognition by elaborate rational-
ization and semantic confusion."[10] Nevertheless, even
with the absence of exhaustive empirical findings, there
is considerable circumstantial evidence that supports the
netherworld thesis. The contention is simply put: Personnel operations at all levels of the public service are
frequently in violation of civil service laws and regulations. This state of affairs is the result of the partisan concerns of politicians as well as the managerial interests of public executives, with the full cooperation

or collusion of the professional personnel operatives. Appropriately, this total process operates in a netherworld; neither openly nor secretly, but in the shadows, similar to a black market. In both instances operations typically continue without serious interference despite the obviousness of their illegality and a surfeit of condemning rhetoric.

All netherworlds arise to fill a genuine social need. The most common example of a political netherworld is the traditionally styled political machine. Robert Merton's analysis of the latent functions of the political machine offers a striking parallel for the contemporary practice of public personnel management. Merton observes that it is the structural context of government "which makes it difficult, if not impossible, for morally approved structures to fulfill essential social functions."[11] The political machine with its marginal concern for traditional morality can perform a variety of social functions that are legally forbidden to conventional governmental structures. Similarly, the officially sanctioned operating procedures of the civil service merit system do not allow many public executives the degree of freedom of action that they feel to be essential for the fulfillment of their administrative and political responsibilities. Following Merton's logic, the needs of public executives would be unsatisfied except for the latent functions of a political machine, or in this case the manifest functions of a public personnel netherworld.

Managers all too frequently find it impossible to fulfill their mandates by fully abiding by the structural constraints of the civil service system. However, since the public manager is in a position to command and/or influence an appropriate fudging of the system, the fudge is made by his personnel functionaires. Such netherworld products take forms suitable to the exigencies of the situation, for example, the otherwise undeserving reallocation of a position to a higher grade level, the exceptional lowering of the passpoint on a promotional exam in order to pick up a favored candidate, or the easing of the qualifications required for a particular position. The netherworld products vary with the special requirements of any given jurisdiction. The public manager, being the customer of these specially made products, pays for them either negatively, by not imposing sanctions of some kind upon the personnel office, or positively, by providing individual rewards for the personnelists or granting additional resources for the other operations of the personnel office. A formal approach bound by the "system" would not allow the manager the flexibility that he demands. In sum, since he can command the resources to, in effect, "buy" the products that he needs for the accomplishment of his mission, a black market of sorts--a netherworld--grows up to serve him.

There is little incentive for elective and appointive public managers to strive to reform the administrative system that nurtures the netherworld. Since they tend to be short-termers, compared to the career officials in the civil service systems, there is little payoff for them to concern themselves with the broad issues of personnel management. Therefore, while their substantive program accomplishments may be significant, their impact on or interest in the manpower posture of their respective agencies tends to be inconsequential. Generally, their only interest in the personnel system is to use it for their short-term benefit. When they are confronted with a constraining personnel system, they have the option of two possible stances or variations thereof. They can choose to operate within these constraints and possibly damage their programs. Alternatively they can approach the constraining system as an adversary to be thwarted. The object is to beat the personnel department at its own game. It has frequently been observed that those administrators viewing their responsibilities as a game tend both to enjoy and to be more successful at their tasks.[12] Typically the opening move in this battle of wits with the personnel office is a resort to bluff and bluster. The personnel office is ordered to do this or that. The director of personnel is impressed with how close the executive is to the mayor, the governor, or the president. When the personnel office begins to balk at the forthcoming anti-merit system reccommendations, the battle is escalated. The director of personnel is asked if he wants to be part of the management team. The executive lets it be known that he suspects certain unnamed individuals of sabotaging his programs. After the manager has exhausted all avenues of threat, bluff, and intimidation, the next stage of play is reached. Hereafter, when occasion demands, the facts of the situation are simply misrepresented. The personnel operative can only act upon what he is officially told; thus, he tends to become an involuntary but knowing accomplice in a public fraud. The position classification process has been heavily abused in this manner.[13] It is a common practice for the requirements of a particular position to be tailored to fit the backgrounds of political and/or otherwise well-connected appointees.[14] In complaining about promotion procedures, a NASA personnel officer is quoted as saying, "The frustration seems to arise not so much from a feeling that the selections made are not good, but that there is a <u>dishonest</u> amount of ritual about the process."[15] In a study of government employee perceptions of their organizational climate in an agency where the personnel rituals were, for the most part, taken seriously, the promotion process "was viewed as one not based on performance and merit," and supervisory level employees "did not view themselves as making a significant input to the promotion process."[16] Not surprisingly it has frequently been observed in a wide variety of jurisdictions that "the most capable managers . . . devote much of their effort and ingenuity to subverting and bypassing the [civil service] regulations."[17] Even the Job Evaluation and Pay Review Task Force to the U.S. Civil Service Commission noted that "present personnel systems do not adequately recognize the value of providing to agency heads a reasonable number of 'their own men' to serve as advocates. This is not necessarily a partisan issue, but it is essential to building a unified and harmonious management team."[18]

The mechanisms of the netherworld are essentially subterfuge devices. Dalton E. McFarland maintains that the "purpose of any subterfuge device is to cover up the real nature of the organization, presenting a more acceptable or more widely appealing front."[19] The "front" in this case is the guise of respectability that covers the administration of civil service programs. Occasionally, however, the guise fades away, such as when periodic allegations of abuses rise to the surface. This has recently happened with the federal government. Mike Causey, a columnist for the Washington <u>Post</u>, has reported that applicants for new positions as well as for promotions in several federal departments were "asked flatly by bosses whether they were registered Republicans or Democrats."[20] In testifying before the House Post Office and Civil Service Committee, Bernard L. Gladieux, Chairman of the Board of Directors of the National Civil Service League, stated:

> It is common knowledge in the Federal community that a rigid political clearance process is now operated by White House staff, extending not only to presidential appointees, for whom such requirements of political loyalty are wholly acceptable, but applying as well as to super-grade appointees and at times even reaching down into lower levels of the civil service.[21]

Believing in the pervasiveness of unwarranted political clearances, the entire board of directors of the non-partisan National Civil Service League issued a special policy statement on the subject:

> Were belief in the existence of political clearance requirements confined to a partisan few, the problem might be readily discounted. Such a conviction, however, is shared by men of probity in and out of government, men of lengthy Washington experience who, in many cases, have direct knowledge of instances of this kind of abuse.[22]

This statement seems to be indirectly confirmed by Roger W. Jones, a former chairman of the U.S. Civil Service Commission and presently a consultant to the Office of Management and Budget, when in discussing his ideal of a personnel policy, he calls for "clearly defined merit systems."[23] Further evidence of the seriousness and pervasiveness of this problem is provided by a survey of the members of the National Capital Area Chapter of the American Society for Public Administration. Almost 73 percent of the members viewed a prospective investigation of charges of political clearance in the career civil service as "very important" or "important."[24]

Direct evidence of such abuses is necessarily spotty. Investigative reporting by the news media is naturally confined to "big" issues; the quiet erosion of the merit system principles, with its protective "veil of ennui," easily goes unobserved. Most scholars, for the reasons previously discussed, tend to ignore this subject. The comparative few having an intimate knowledge of the personnel netherworld know that the disclosure of such machinations would only limit the organizational access necessary for their more traditional research; it would also limit their lucrative consultantships.

Yet in spite of these inhibitors, the specific facts on abuses occasionally rise to the surface. Most recently the Department of Housing and Urban Development has been accused of "violating the law by appointing political favorites to career civil service jobs."[25] But it is unfair to label one department as delinquent when almost all the others have a culpability differing only in degree. Bernard Rosen, the executive director of the U.S. Civil Service Commission, publicly announced to a meeting of governmental administrators that "hiring officials have been breaking the law--as much as if they embezzled federal funds--by taking job shortcuts." According to Rosen because "too many federal officials view merit regulations as an obstacle to placing the best people quickly in jobs . . . rule-breaking in that area isn't considered serious by many of the brass."[26] However, Rosen would undoubtedly disagree with Nathan Wolkomir, head of the National Federation of Federal Employees, who asserts that "mere pious lip service" is now paid to the merit system.[27] The veracity of Wolkomir's assertion varies on a continuum from generally true to generally false depending upon which federal agency is being discussed.

While it is a hopeful sign that the U.S. Civil Service Commission has recognized the general tendency of public executives to garner administrative discretion by violating constraining regulations, the commission's views of such violations are reminiscent of the federal government's attitude toward prohibition. In both cases the government sought to forbid by simple fiat behavior patterns that had not only existed for centuries, but represented qualities generally admired in the overall culture as well. Just as western culture grudgingly respects the man who can "hold his liquor," or "drinks everybody under the table," so too, we admire personal loyalty, the man who can break through red tape, and the ability to accomplish an assignment against all obstacles. Prohibition was repealed because it proved to be unenforceable. It does not seem unreasonable to suggest that many merit system provisions will eventually be repealed after it becomes commonly recognized that they, too, are unenforceable. As Fritz Morstein Marx has observed, "legislation cannot banish either the astute spoilsman or the single-minded official who is set to get around particular requirements of civil service law."[28] An official determined to have his way with personnel matters tends to invoke the "canons of managerial freedom to juggle things about for his own reasons, often with the help of career men who do not mind being 'realistic' about these matters."[29]

But Marx begs the significant question of why the career men, the personnel operatives, are so willing to be "realistic." Certainly the various merit systems could not be manipulated so easily without the technical expertise of the personnel establishment. Public managers would hardly be able to use the personnel process as they do were it not for what Chester I. Barnard, in his classic Functions of the Executive, termed the "zone of indifference."

If all the orders for actions reasonably practicable be arranged in the order of their acceptability to the person affected, it may be conceived that there are a number which are clearly unacceptable, that is, which certainly will not be obeyed; there is another group somewhat more or less on the neutral line, that is, either barely acceptable or barely unacceptable; and a third group unquestionably acceptable. This last group lies within the "zone of indifference." The person affected will accept orders lying within this zone and is relatively indifferent as to what the order is so far as the question of authority is concerned.[30]

Public officials are commonly in the dubious legal and moral position of conspiring with their personnel operatives to misrepresent facts and events to civil service commissions, the jurisdictions' employees, and to the public. For example, a job vacancy may be announced as open to all when, in reality, a candidate has been preselected; or a promotion may be justified on merit when the only thing meritorious about the employee may be his political sponsorship. Personnel directors and their staffs tend to assist in these perversions of their established merit systems because such actions are acceptable to them. Such actions are within their "zone of indifference." This is not to say that personnel people will do absolutely anything that their superiors wish. Some things are just too gross. Clericals cannot generally be made into supergrades; but a law graduate with practically no professional experience can be if his other credentials--read political endorsements--are appropriate.

A personnelist's "zone of indifference" shrinks and expands according to his perceptions of the legitimacy of his orders. Career bureaucrats tend to give elected and appointed officials the benefit of any doubt they may have over the extent of their authority. To do less would be to reject the fundamental democratic notion of political control. "Subordinate compliance is thus a pillar of democratic government."[31] Is that compliance equally democratic when it requires the violation of legislative and judicial mandates? What may be obvious in a philosophy seminar is not so easy in practice. Considerable evidence exists that subordinates in American civilian and military bureaucracies will violate a variety of moral and legal provisions rather than disobey their superiors.[32] Unfortunately, the same can be said for the rest of society.[33]

The leading occupational hazard of public personnel operatives is an enlarged "zone of indifference." The main symptom of this problem is a chronic cynicism addressed mainly to personnel functions, but frequently extending to the whole panoply of public administration. The long-term prognosis is for increasing pressures on the conscience to the point of numbness[34] and the development of a negative self-image. According to the report on a symposium of young personnel professionals held at the Federal Executive Institute, cynicism "has all too often been the common feeling among personnel people about their work."[35] The symposium noted that the basic medium of communication and identification among personnelists "has been a sharing of horror stories, a 'can you top this' of frustrations and disappointments of the personnel administration 'game.'"[36] The basic cause of this disabling cynicism is the disparity between what the personnelist desires to be in his organization and the role that is foisted upon him. This disparity, leading to a poor self-image, is compensated in part by the development of cynical attitudes toward his work.

Empirical evidence of the deprecatory self-image of the personnelist is provided by a survey of the self-perceptions of personnel administrators. Francis L. Harmon asked 120 federal personnel officers in grades GS-11 to GS-16 to identify traits associated with both the "ideal" and "typical" personnel officer. Harmon concluded that the typical personnel officer views himself as a good organization man. "He strives to please by conforming to the wishes and expectations of his associates, and to the demands of the organization. He does what he is told . . . above all, he is cautious of independent thinking, which might lead to boat rocking innovations."[37] In stark contrast the ideal personnel officer is seen as a professional of high caliber. "He receives the attention and respect, if not the liking, to which his professional training and skill entitle him. He can be a leader, an innovator, because he can speak out with authority, and is not loath to do so when the occasion requires it."[38]

Unfortunately, the expertise generally extant in personnel offices tends to be limited to a knowledge of civil service procedures. Consequently, this does not develop into the kind of power that is the prerogative of experts in other fields.[39] Since a professional's authority is premised upon a claim to unique or superior competency in a specialized area of knowledge, "the personnel occupations have only tenuous claims to exclusive expertise."[40] As a result the personnel officer's true role is far from the idealized model of the respected professional being listened to by top management because of the authority embodied in his expertise.[41]

The idealized professional role that many personnel operatives try so hard to believe in is an occupational myth—a development not uncommon in low-status occupations. "These myths serve the function of enhancing the status of the occupation, at least in the eyes of the individual involved."[42] Common examples are the psychiatric ward attendant who views his primary responsibility as the care of the patients;[43] or the night watchman who views himself as a managerial representative.[44] It is through the development of such myths that the occupation "becomes more palatable and commitment becomes possible."[45]

Why is there so little resistance to netherworld operations on the part of personnelists? Why do they seem to be such willing accomplices in activities that they know to be so ethically dubious? The answer is to be found by examining the tangential consequences of their lack of professionalism. Personnel, while an ancient function, is a comparatively recent occupation. It was during the period between the two world wars that personnel emerged as a permanent occupational specialty in both industry and government.[46] The various federal departments have only had formal divisions of personnel since 1938.[47] Personnel has not yet been fleshed out as a profession. People are attracted to personnel work by expediency and not by a premeditated decision to undertake years of specialized training in preparation for a life's work. The great majority of personnel operatives enter the field, not because of a long-standing desire to be a personnel person, but because a personnel position was open to them when they happened to need a job.[48] Consequently, their orientation toward the employing organization differs markedly from that exhibited by true professionals.

Alvin W. Gouldner, the well-known sociologist, has identified two latent social roles that manifest themselves in organizational settings. The first role, that of a "cosmopolitan," tends to be adopted by true professionals. It assumes a small degree of loyalty to the employing organization, a high commitment to specialized skills, and an outer reference group orientation. The second role, that of a "local," tends to be adopted by nonprofessionals. It assumes a high degree of loyalty to the employing organization, a low commitment to specialized skills, and an inner reference group orientation.[49] While these role models are extremes and represent the two ends of a continuum, they go far to explain why personnel operatives tend to be so compliant with nether world operations. Not being true professionals, their loyalty lies not with professional and ethical obligations but with their immediate organization. There is little sense of commitment to specialized skills or to reference groups outside the immediate organization. Indeed, their immediate organization is their reference group; and it is from this group that the personnelist takes his behavior cues. The pull that any sense of professionalism has on him is so slight that it can neither prevent him from conspiring to pervert the merit system regulations nor comfort him if he resists. "Unable to commit himself to his occupation, the personnel manager must commit himself to the organization in order to make his work life meaningful and satisfactory."[50] Personnel operatives tend to make this organizational commitment "because the occupation has no real substance with which to identify."[51]

The poor relationship that usually exists between top management and the personnel office contributes to the cynicism and associated malaise of the personnelists. Personnel administration has seldom been a fully integrated part of the management process in the public service. In spite of protestations to the contrary, the personnel function has continued to be a subordinate staff function. According to the present chairman of the U.S. Civil Service Commission, Robert Hampton, the "average manager does not call his personnel officer for advice until he's got a major fire on his hands."[52] The personnel officer "is not as privy to the policy councils as he should be."[53] Further evidence of this is supplied by a study of the role of the personnel director in Michigan state government. The major finding of this state-sponsored report was that the "personnel director's decision making role was an advisory one."[54] Personnel directors, looking to the ideal, desired department heads to delegate personnel policy decisions totally to them.[55] That this is seldom done in actuality indicates that personnel policy decisions are considered too important to be left to the personnel directors. Under present conditions--quite rightly so.

Because personnel is not treated as an equal member of the management team, and has a decided and obvious second-class status, there is seldom the mutuality of respect that is essential to healthy viable relationships.

The primary function of an effective manager is
to promote and enhance appropriate and adaptive
behavior on the part of those persons interacting
with him. This requires an ability to manipulate people but in such a way that neither individual is deceived nor made to feel less human
in that interaction.[56]

Personnel is typically treated exactly to the contrary. One writer using an anthropological metaphor has
appropriately characterized the personnel office as a
group of squaw-men--those members of a primitive tribe
that are relegated to remaining around the campsite with
the women while the men go off and hunt.[57] While not
wholly accurate, there is enough truth in this imagery for
it to be embarrassingly familiar. With employees who will
tolerate such working conditions, the result is professional ineffectuality; with employees who will not tolerate such conditions, the result is turnover.[58]

Why has the personnel operative been called an "administrative harlot?" Public managers have long been asking
their personnel officers to do things that they would not
normally ask their wives to do. On a routine basis public
personnel operatives are required to lie, cheat, and otherwise pervert the civil service regulations that they and
the elected and appointed officials above them are legally
obligated to uphold. In one sense all personnelists are
latent prostitutes. They never know when the crunch will
come, when a change in top leadership will force them to
perform acts they would not otherwise consider. Of course,
this is a generalization that could apply to all management positions. But personnel operations are significantly
different from the other processes of management in that
the scope of personnel activities is rigidly prescribed
by civil service regulations. A common retort to this
statement would be to reassert the value of "flexibility."[59]
But when a group of young personnel professionals met at
the Federal Executive Institute to discuss this problem,
they viewed this much vaunted "flexibility" as "cheating,
thereby robbing personnel of its effectiveness and personnelists of their self-respect."[60]

While personnelists engage in their own special genre
of harlotry, they perform many of the same social functions
and exhibit some of the same emotional symptoms as conventional prostitutes. Consequently, relating the self-image
of the personnelist to that of the prostitute has more justification to it on the part of personnelists than self-

pity, and more justification on the part of the author
than mere literary license.[61] Both are service occupations
that, depending upon the jurisdictional location, perform
marginally legal or illegal "safety valve" functions for
society. Thus, they help preserve the status quo. While
their actions obviously deviate from traditional norms,
they "have the long-term function of supporting conform-
ity."[62] Just as prostitutes accommodate the sexual frustrations of society, the personnelist through his legal,
quasi-legal, and illegal massaging of the civil service
system keeps the lid on--prevents the legitimate and illegitimate demands on the system from reaching the exploding
point. As with prostitution and other illegal professions,
the latent function of the personnelist is to handle the
unsolved problems and dilemmas "which may burden individuals within the existing social system."[63] Thus, if an
elected public executive finds that he cannot live within
the constraints of the civil service system with which he
is burdened, he can discuss his problems with his personnel operatives. There is usually something a director of
personnel can do to provide at least temporary relief for
administrative suffering due to the constraints of civil
service regulations. If nothing else, he can always resort to the old temporary employee gambit.

Most jurisdictions are legally prohibited from hiring
temporary or provisional employees for more than three,
six, or nine months.[64] The federal government has a one-
year limit on temporary employees. It is obviously an
abuse of the merit system to simply and automatically rehire
an employee after the expiration of his temporary employment period. Yet, as in the Denmark of old, some things
are "more honour'd in the breach than the observance."[65]
It is estimated that nearly 40 percent of Chicago's public
employees were classified as "temporaries," meaning that
they may hold jobs for no more than 180 days. "Some politically active employees have held these 180-day temporary
jobs for twenty years after getting appointed and reap-
pointed."[66] Toward the end of Mayor Lindsay's administration, New York City had about 30,000 provisional appointees.[67] A New York State commission investigating governmental operations in New York City found that 83 percent
of almost 1,000 employees in one agency alone had held
their temporary jobs for periods beyond the nine-month civil
service limitation--some for as long as seven years.[68]
Just as the political community supports organized crime
and a variety of illegal activities on the part of its government,[69] there is nothing systemically illegitimate about

maintaining a public personnel netherworld. Indeed, there is considerable precedent for awarding public employment advantages to such special groups as veterans and minorities. What is so contemptible about the public personnel netherworld is not its operations, which are frequently benign, but its hypocrisy.

It might seem to those involved with public personnel operations that some outrageous things have been said here; but nothing has been said that does not befit an outrageous situation. Ever mindful that truth is the only defense for accusations of libel, the author is naturally cautious about pushing his analogies too far.[70] Many personnel officials are deserving of great respect from the public; others deserve pity; still others, contempt. The comparison of personnelists with prostitutes is done solely for the purposes of lucidity; it is not intended to be gratuitously offensive. Many personnelists will have found the substantive issues of this discussion offensive enough.

The netherworld of public personnel administration is more than just another informal organizational mechanism working to complement the formal structure by compensating for its shortcomings. It is an insidious cancer that quietly and relentlessly erodes the budding professionalism and spirit of the personnel establishment. In addition to whatever trauma it causes for the participants in its dramas,[71] it serves to subvert the democratic processes of government by institutionalizing a system of governance that is neither known by the public nor formally sanctioned by their elected representatives. For example, by inviting applicants to apply for positions when a candidate has already been preselected, the netherworld perpetuates a fraud upon the public, thus extending its infectious malaise of cynicism to the citizenry. While organizational and party politics will always be with us, there is no appropriate place for this kind of institutionalized hypocrisy in the public bureaucracies of the United States. Actually, the amount of hypocrisy in public personnel operations probably compares favorably to that exhibited by industrial personnel operations and other managerial functions, but there is a crucial difference. Public personnel hypocrisies are forbidden by law.

NOTES

1. Statement of Robert Vaughn, Assistant Professor of Law, the American University, <u>Hearings Legislative Over-</u>

sight Review of the Civil Service Commission, Subcommittee on Investigations of the Committee on Post Office and Civil Service, 92d Cong., 2d Sess., House serial no. 92-54 (Washington, D.C., September 26, 1972), p. 26.

2. Robert D. Miewald, "On Teaching Public Personnel Administration--A Weberian Perspective," Western Political Quarterly 26 (March 1973): 97.

3. Gerald E. Caiden, "Public Personnel Administration in the Doldrums?" Public Personnel Review 32 (January 1971): 30-35.

4. Heinz Eulau, "A Note on the Discipline: Que Vadimus?" P.S.: Newsletter of the American Political Science Association (Winter 1969), p. 12. This situation may be changing with the tightening academic job market of the 1970s. As Dwight Waldo observes, "Unlike most branches of political science, the study of personnel administration produces a salable skill." The Administrative State (New York: Ronald Press, 1948), p. 27.

5. Miewald, "On Teaching Public Personnel Administration," p. 98.

6. Paul P. Van Riper, "Public Personnel Literature: The Last Decade," Public Personnel Review 22 (October 1961): 231.

7. Two examples: O. Glenn Stahl, Public Personnel Administration, 6th ed. (New York: Harper & Row, 1971); Robert T. Golembiewski and Michael Cohen, eds., People in Public Service: A Reader in Public Personnel Administration (Itasca, Ill.: F. E. Peacock Publishers, 1970).

8. New York Times Magazine, October 28, 1973, p. 91.

9. The prime reasons that so little of this material comes to light have always been obvious. Writing in 1938 Lewis Meriam observed that the most valuable case materials for the study of public personnel administration were "so highly confidential that they are skeletons in the official closet and the administrator must be closed mouth about them." Public Personnel Problems from the Standpoint of the Operating Officer (Washington, D.C.: Brookings Institution, 1938), p. 12.

10. Husain Mustafa and Anthony A. Salomone, "Administrative Circumvention of Public Policy," Midwest Review of Public Administration 5, no. 1 (1971): 17.

11. Robert K. Merton, Social Theory and Social Structure, rev. ed. (Glencoe, Ill.: The Free Press of Glencoe, 1957), p. 72.

12. For a discussion of this outside the context of personnel, see John Relfuss, Public Administration as Political Process (New York: Charles Scribner's Sons, 1973), p. 3.

13. For a detailed description of how the classification process is abused in this manner, see Jay M. Shafritz, Position Classification: A Behavioral Analysis for the Public Service (New York: Praeger, 1973), ch. 5, "Philadelphia as a Case Study."

14. New York City follows a similar pattern. New York Times, October 18, 1972, p. 51. That this same phenomenon exists in the federal service has been admitted by the executive director of the U.S. Civil Service Commission. Washington Post, December 3, 1973, p. B13.

15. Judson Gooding, The Job Revolution (New York: Walker, 1972), p. 31.

16. Robert K. Wagner, An Investigation of Government Employee Perceptions of Their Organizational Climate (Washington, D.C.: U.S. Department of Commerce, National Technical Information Service no. AD-735352, December 1971), pp. 75-76.

17. E. S. Savas and Sigmund G. Ginsburg, "The Civil Service: A Meritless System," Public Interest 32 (Summer 1973): 74. This article is mainly a witty and devastating attack on the New York City civil service system.

18. Report of the Job Evaluation and Pay Review Task Force to the United States Civil Service Commission, Committee on Post Office and Civil Service, Subcommittee on Employee Benefits, 92d Cong., 2d Sess., House Committee print no. 16 (Washington, D.C.: U.S. Government Printing Office, January 12, 1972), vol. 2, p. 9. This report is popularly known as the Oliver Report after the director of the task force, Philip M. Oliver.

19. Dalton E. McFarland, Cooperation and Conflict in Personnel Administration (New York: American Foundation for Management Research, 1962), p. 122. Even though McFarland is examining private industry, he found that "the personnel department frequently experiences the phenomenon of organizational subterfuge."

20. Washington Post, May 4, 1973, p. D17.

21. Statement before the House Committee on Post Office and Civil Service concerning S. 1682, April 25, 1972, as quoted by Robert Vaughn in Hearings, Legislative Oversight Review of the Civil Service Commission, p. 16.

22. This was published in the June 1973 National Capital Area Chapter, American Society for Public Administration, NCAC-ASPA Newsletter.

23. "Future Trends in Public Administration--Predictions and Dreams," ASPA News & Views 24 (January 1974): 6.

24. NCAC-ASPA Newsletter, May 1973, p. 6.

25. New York Times, November 11, 1973, p. 1.

26. The direct quotes are Mike Causey's paraphrasing of Bernard Rosen's remarks. Washington Post, December 3, 1973, p. B13.

27. Statement of Nathan T. Wolkomir, quoted by Henry W. Messaros in the Philadelphia Bulletin, July 15, 1973, Section 2, p. 6.

28. Fritz Morstein Marx, The Administrative State: An Introduction to Bureaucracy (Chicago: University of Chicago Press, 1957), p. 75.

29. Ibid.

30. Chester I. Barnard, The Function of the Executive, 30th anniversary ed. (Cambridge, Mass.: Harvard University Press, 1966), pp. 168-69.

31. Herbert Kaufman, Administrative Feedback in Monitoring Subordinates' Behavior (Washington, D.C.: Brookings Institution, 1973), p. 4. A further discussion of this can be found in Lewis C. Mainzer, Political Bureaucracy (Glenview, Ill.: Scott, Foresman & Co., 1973), pp. 72-76.

32. For overwhelming evidence of this one need only examine the myriad facets of the Watergate scandals or the large variety of illegal and unauthorized bombings in Indochina. For general accounts of governmental lying, see David Wise, The Politics of Lying: Government, Deception, Secrecy, and Power (New York: Random House, 1973); Anthony Lake, "Lying Around Washington," Foreign Policy, no. 2 (Spring 1971).

33. For a summary of experiments that overwhelmingly demonstrate the propensity of individuals to obey authority figures despite the obvious immorality and cruelty of their acts, see Stanley Milgram, Obedience to Authority: An Experimental View (New York: Harper & Row, 1973).

34. The immoral premises of many personnel practices are due in part to the "lack of internal sensitivity to the existence of any moral dilemmas that might be of concern to practitioners. Bureaucrats are finely tuned by their training to avoid discomfiting moral questions." Eugene P. Dvorin and Robert H. Simmons, From Amoral to Human Bureaucracy (New York: Canfield Press, Harper & Row, 1972), p. 63.

35. Report of the Symposium of Young Personnel Professionals (Charlottesville, Va.: Federal Executive Institute, July 1970), p. 2.

36. Ibid. Unfortunately this problem goes beyond the personnel office. According to O. Glenn Stahl, "persons with high ideals are alienated from government in general if their experience in government employment leaves them frustrated and cynical." O. Glenn Stahl, "What the Person-

nel Function Is All About," <u>Civil Service Journal</u> 12 (July-September 1971): 12. For an excellent anthology of illegal and unethical behavior in government, see Theodore L. Becker and Vernon G. Murray, eds., <u>Government Lawlessness in America</u> (New York: Oxford University Press, 1971).

37. Francis L. Harmon, <u>The Personnel Officer: A Self-Image</u> (Unpublished report of the Personnel Research Staff of the U.S. Department of Agriculture, 1965), p. 8. This study is available in the library of the U.S. Civil Service Commission.

38. Ibid.

39. For a discussion of how experts acquire power and thus influence, see Guy Benveniste, <u>The Politics of Expertise</u> (Berkeley, Calif.: The Glendessary Press, 1972), ch. 7.

40. George Ritzer and Harrison M. Trice, <u>An Occupation in Conflict: A Study of the Personnel Manager</u> (Ithaca: New York State School of Industrial and Labor Relations, Cornell University, 1969), p. 28.

41. For an analysis of the personnel officer's role in the traditional manner of the behavioralists, see Geoffrey Y. Cornog, "The Personnel Administrator: His Role and His Role Conflicts," in Robert T. Golembiewski, Frank Gibson, and Geoffrey Cornog, eds., <u>Public Administration: Readings in Institutions, Processes, Behavior</u>, 2d ed. (Chicago: Rand McNally, 1972), pp. 76-89.

42. Ritzer and Trice, <u>An Occupation in Conflict</u>, p. 41. A survey of 160 federal personnel administrators, grades GS-9 through GS-13, in Atlanta, Georgia, found that they showed a preference for an idealistic view of the agency environment. William A. Jones, <u>Federal Personnel Administrators in a Regional City: A Study in Occupational Perceptions</u> (D.P.A. dissertation, University of Georgia, 1972).

43. Richard Simpson and Ida Simpson, "The Psychiatric Attendant: Development of an Occupational Self Image in a Low Status Occupation," <u>American Sociological Review</u> 24 (1959): 389-93, as cited in Ritzer and Trice, <u>An Occupation in Conflict</u>, p. 41.

44. H. M. Trice, "Night Watchmen: A Study of an Isolated Occupation," <u>I.L.R. Research</u> 10, no. 2 (1960): 3-9, as cited in Ritzer and Trice, <u>An Occupation in Conflict</u>, p. 42.

45. Ritzer and Trice, <u>An Occupation in Conflict</u>, p. 42.

46. For histories of the development of personnel as an occupation, see Gerald E. Kahler and Alton C. Johnson, <u>The Development of Personnel Administration, 1923-1945</u>

(Madison: University of Wisconsin, Graduate School of Business, Bureau of Business Research and Service, Monograph no. 3, January 1971); Cyril Curtis Ling, The Management of Personnel Relations: History and Origins (Homewood, Ill.: Richard D. Irwin, 1965).

47. World War II gave a great impetus to personnel administration in the federal service. See Gladys M. Kammerer, Impact of War on Federal Personnel Administration, 1939-1945 (Lexington: University of Kentucky Press, 1951).

48. A variety of studies have confirmed this. See Albert P. Maslow, The Federal Personnel Man: A Survey of the Occupation, the People, the Work Environment (Washington, D.C.: U.S. Civil Service Commission, Bureau of Policies and Standards, Survey Item no. 35, September 1966); Ritzer and Trice, An Occupation in Conflict, p. 35; Jay M. Shafritz, The Municipal Middle Management System in Philadelphia (Ph.D. dissertation, Temple University, 1971), p. 203.

49. Alvin W. Gouldner, "Cosmopolitans and Locals: Toward an Analysis of Latent Social Roles--I," Administrative Science Quarterly 2 (December 1957): 290. While Gouldner's construct has received substantial empirical testing and criticisms, its value as a general model remains evident. For a critical examination of the construct, see Andrew J. Grimes and Philip K. Berger, "Cosmopolitan-Local: Evaluation of a Construct," Administrative Science Quarterly 15 (December 1970): 407-16.

50. Ritzer and Trice, An Occupation in Conflict, p. 43.

51. Ibid.

52. Robert Hampton, "Conversation with the Chairman," Civil Service Journal 9 (April-June 1969): 7. Four years later the Civil Service Commission was saying the same thing. Gilbert A. Schulkind, director of the Bureau of Personnel Management Evaluation, was quoted as saying that managers were bypassing personnel officers "as the experts in matters involving personnel management." Len Famiglietti, "Personnel Officers Subject of Review," Federal Times, January 17, 1973, p. 1.

53. Hampton, Conversation with the Chairman," p. 7.

54. Mary K. Rothman, The Role of the Personnel Director in Michigan State Government (Report of the Office of Program and Performance Evaluation and Audit of the Michigan Department of Civil Service, June 1972), p. 63.

55. Ibid.

56. Arthur Whatley and Larry Schieffer, "Therapeutic Relationships in Management: Thesis or Antithesis to Man-

agement Success?" <u>S.A.M. Advanced Management Journal</u> 38 (January 1973): 52.

57. Stephen M. Sweeney, "Squaw-Man in the Personnel Department," <u>Personnel Journal</u> 51 (December 1972): 888. Sweeney derives his term "squaw-man" from Anthony Jay, <u>Corporation Man</u> (New York: Random House, 1971).

58. For a book-length discussion of turnover that addresses itself to dead-end or "doomsday" jobs, see Dean B. Peskin, <u>The Doomsday Job: The Behavioral Anatomy of Turnover</u> (New York: AMACOM, 1973).

59. For a handbook on legitimate flexibilities in the federal personnel system, see U.S. Civil Service Commission, <u>How to Make the Most of the Merit System: Understanding and Using Flexibilities in the Federal Personnel System</u> (Washington, D.C.: U.S. Government Printing Office, February 1968).

60. <u>Report of the Symposium of Young Personnel Professionals</u>, p. 11. In this regard it is worth observing that integrity seems to be an extremely important commodity to personnel administrators. A survey of 861 members of the American Society for Personnel Administration determined that the participants felt that the single most distinctive trait necessary for top personnel positions was integrity. Richard P. Calhoon and L. Frederick Van Eck, Jr., <u>An Analytical Study of Requirements for Top Positions in Personnel Administration</u> (Chapel Hill: University of North Carolina, Graduate School of Business Administration, Research Paper 12, February 1964), p. 15. The survey also included members of the International Association of Personnel Women. Two-thirds of the respondents felt integrity was the most crucial trait. The next most mentioned trait was objectivity, which was listed by only two-fifths of the respondents.

61. The author's notions of personnel prostitution did not originate with him but with some anonymous personnel department staff member who, during a moment of exasperation several years ago, said in the presence of the author, "All we do around here is prostitute ourselves." Such a statement really made an impression upon a young man considering personnel as a vocation.

62. Elliott A. Krause, <u>The Sociology of Occupations</u> (Boston: Little, Brown & Co., 1971), p. 290. See chapter 11, "Illegal Occupations," pp. 279-95.

63. Ibid., p. 290.

64. For example, Philadelphia has a three-month limit; Chicago, six months; New York, nine months.

65. William Shakespeare, <u>Hamlet</u>, Act I, Scene 4.

66. Martin and Susan Tolchin, <u>To the Victor: Politi-</u> <u>cal Patronage from the Clubhouse to the White House</u> (New York: Vintage Books, 1971), pp. 40-41.

67. New York <u>Times</u>, October 16, 1972, p. 19.

68. Ibid., October 22, 1972, p. 30; January 31, 1973, p. 45.

69. Community sanctioned illegal activities on the part of government officials have long been a part of American political tradition. Innumerable studies support the continuity of this tradition. For example, in his autobiography Lincoln Steffens recounts his discussing with a group of businessmen the impossibility of engaging in a significant enterprise "without corrupting or joining in the corruption of the government." <u>Autobiography of Lincoln Steffens</u> (Chautauqua, N.Y.: Chautauqua Press, 1931), pp. 572-73. Several generations later the same phenomenon is observed when the New York City Department of Investigation reports that "not a building is built nor a structure renovated without the payment of as much as tens of thousands of dollars to government and union officials." Harlow Unger, "Bribes Expedite All N.Y. Building," <u>Washington Post</u>, August 27, 1972, p. F1.

70. It is easy and cheap to take great liberties with this analogy to prostitution, and the author is trying mightily to control his puckish inclinations.

71. In regard to trauma, a strong case could be made that public personnel units, because of the pressure of living on the interface between nether and other worlds, tend to be neurotic organizations. For a discussion of this phenomenon, see Jerry B. Harvey and D. Richard Albertson, "Neurotic Organizations: Symptoms, Causes and Treatment," <u>Personnel Journal</u> 50 (September 1971): 694-99.

8

POLITICAL CULTURE—
THE DETERMINANT OF
MERIT SYSTEM
VIABILITY

Public personnel management is constantly being judged in the wrong context. It is erroneously viewed as a public sector counterpart to industrial management systems. However, the private sector analogy holds true only for a portion of the total public personnel function, and the size of that portion depends on the degree to which the jurisdiction is politicized. Thus, public personnel operations cannot be properly understood or evaluated outside the political context of the host jurisdiction.

The determinant of any community's attitudes toward the quality and vigor of the jurisdiction's personnel operation is the political culture of the geographic area concerned. Even Thomas Jefferson observed that "some states require a different regimen from others."[1] Indeed, the only way to find an explanation for the extreme variations of the quality or vigor of American civil service systems is to examine the cultural context of American governmental units. In recent years there has been considerable discussion of the cultural dimensions associated with the administration of programs by and for minority groups, such as blacks, American Indians, and Mexican-Americans.[2] Yet little has appeared concerning the impact of the larger American political culture on the administrative processes of government. While some textbooks on public administration and organizational behavior contain chapters on the cultural background of organizations, they tend to take an anthropological and/or sociological approach to the subject.[3] The political determinants of organizational culture are generally not considered.[4]

The quality of public personnel operations varies for a variety of reasons. A significant contributor to variations in operations is the substantial disagreement as to just what constitutes a quality operation. While some zealots advocate the tightest possible merit system mechanisms, others with equal vigor and concern for the efficacy of operations cry out for greater discretion on the part of managers and an eventual dissolution of straitjacket civil service procedures. While honest critics may differ on what constitutes quality personnel programs, one quiet yet domineering fact remains. The quality or style of operations is determined only in the lesser part by well-meaning critics or even by the personnel administrators themselves; the crucial determinant is the political will of the community or jurisdiction as expressed by its political culture and manifest by the administrative style of public programs.

James Q. Wilson has demonstrated that the style of police operations in eight communities reflected not some abstract standard of quality or professionalism but the expressed and/or implied desires of the community.[5] For example, the police were either exceedingly lenient or exceedingly strict with minor legal violations, depending upon the perceived degree of community concern one way or the other. A similar condition exists with personnel operations. Merit systems arrayed along a continuum tend to be tight and legalistic or open to manipulation, reflecting community attitudes. Since public personnel agencies typically have a policing role to perform, it is useful to compare their operating premises to those of police departments in the same jurisdiction. Wilson considers a police department to have a "watchman" style of performance if it is one in which order maintenance is perceived to be the prime function of the department.[6] Such a police operation will tend to ignore law infringements that do not involve "serious" crimes, such as minor traffic violations, bookmaking, and illegal church bingo. Correspondingly, a public personnel agency exhibiting this style might knowingly accept false information as the basis for a position reallocation, might encourage unsuspecting applicants to apply for a job vacancy for which a candidate has been preselected, or might allow the equal rights provisions of recent legislation to be ignored or abused. Of course, all these activities or nonactivities are subject to occasional crackdowns. Just as the police periodically shut down illegal gambling operations in response to the political needs of the police chief or mayor, "watchman" style personnel operations periodically tighten their classification procedures or pump new life into their upward mobility programs in response to the political needs of the appointed or elected executives. The thrust of the "watchman" style in both instances is to maintain order, to insure a smooth, nondisruptive running of the community or bureaucracy. Legal considerations and official operating mandates are paramount only when the "heat" is on. Of course, the standard operating procedures of police or personnel departments will tend to be more legalistic in communities that are so disposed.

While a community's political culture is seldom articulated, it nevertheless serves as a source of definition. By determining the values to be applied to any given problem, the political culture insures that the decisional process is filtered through its value system before administrative action is taken. Just as other aspects of culture create an individual's needs hierarchy by ordering the importance of such things as new clothes, big cars, and ancestor worship in his life, the political culture is a significant influence in establishing an individual's hierarchy of role obligation whereby his legalistic responsibilities are placed above or below his obligations to political party, kinship group, coreligionists, and so forth. It establishes the parameters of the systemically legitimate activities in which an individual may participate without incurring community sanctions. Even when corruption is rife, it is the cultural environment that sets the limits and direction of such corruption. Melvin M. Belli, the noted attorney, relates a story that illustrates this point. Years ago Belli traveled to Paris to represent his client, movie star Errol Flynn, who had a legal tangle with a French firm. When Belli arrived the French lawyer on the case advised him that there was nothing to worry about: "We have given the judge 200,000 francs and the case is in the bag." When Belli wondered aloud what would happen if the other side were to give the judge 300,000 francs, his French associate became indignant and replied, "But Monsieur, he is a French judge--he only takes from one side!"[7]

While passing mention of the importance of the cultural context of public management has long been made by leading organizational theorists,[8] a viable classification of the various American political cultures was not achieved until the mid-1960s with the work of Daniel J. Elazar of Temple University. Elazar arrived at his determinations of the political subcultures of the United States by examining three sets of factors for each locality studied: the sources of political culture, such as race, ethnicity, and religion; the manifestations of political culture, such as political attitudes, behavior, and symbols; and the effects of political culture, such as political actions and public policies.[9] In this manner he was able to identify the political subcultures for each of several hundred American communities.

Elazar views the overall American political culture as consisting of three major subcultures: the individualistic, the moralistic, and the traditionalistic.[10] The individualistic political culture

> holds politics to be just another means by which individuals may improve themselves socially and economically.
>
> The individualistic political culture is ambivalent about the place of bureaucracy in the political order.
>
> The bureaucratic method of operation flies in the face of the favor system that is central to the individualistic political process. . . . Large segments of the bureaucracy may be insulated from it through the merit system but the entire organization is pulled into the political environment at crucial points through political appointment at the upper echelons, and, very frequently, the bending of the merit system to meet political demands.[11]

In the moralistic political culture

> both the general public and the politicians conceive of politics as a public activity centered on some notion of the public good and properly devoted to the advancement of the public interest. Good government, then, is measured by the degree to which it promotes the public good and in terms of the honesty, selflessness, and commitment to the public welfare of those who govern.
>
> The notion of a politically neutral administrative system creates no problem within the moralistic value system and even offers many advantages. Where merit systems are instituted, they tend to be rigidly maintained.[12]

The traditionalistic political culture

reflects an older precommercial attitude that accepts a substantially hierarchical society as part
of the ordered nature of things, authorizing and
expecting those at the top of the social structure
to take a special and dominant role in government.
Traditionalistic political cultures tend to
be instinctively antibureaucratic because bureaucracy by its very nature interferes with the fine
web of informal interpersonal relationships that
lie at the root of the political system and have
been developed by following traditional patterns
over the years. Where bureaucracy is introduced,
it is generally confined to ministerial functions
under the aegis of the established power holders.[13]

Since political culture is essentially a value system,
it can best be understood in terms of the boundaries it
sets for political behavior. "Its influence lies in its
power to set reasonably fixed limits to political behavior
and provide subliminal direction for political action."[14]
The political culture influences the operations of the
larger political system by molding the community's perceptions of the nature and purposes of politics; by influencing
the recruitment of specific kinds of people to become active in government as holders of elective offices, members
of the bureaucracy, and political workers; and by subtly
directing politicians and public officials in the light of
their perceptions.[15]
The study of political culture would seem to offer
great predictive potential for the efficacy of governmental
operations. Thus, one could expect that the inhabitants
of a political culture that viewed public office as essentially a means of personal gain would be unlikely to support
a strong merit system. Conversely, a culture with a high
moral ethic would be unlikely to maintain a spoils system
as regards public office. Table 1 illustrates the kind of
attitude each of Elazar's three political cultures tend to
take toward government bureaucracy and merit systems.
While Elazar's political subculture designations are not
definitive, they do provide a fairly accurate index of the
cultural manifestations that can reasonably be anticipated.
Thus, Minnesota with its overwhelmingly moralistic orientation would be expected to have strong merit systems,[16] while
Chicago with its individualistic orientation would be expected to have an extensive patronage program.[17] Similarly,
the South with its traditionalistic orientation would be
more likely to be hostile to merit system installations than

TABLE 1

Views of Elazar's Three Political Subcultures Toward
Bureaucracy and Merit Systems

	Individualistic	Moralistic	Traditionalistic
View of bureaucracy	Ambivalent (undesirable because it limits favors and patronage, but good because it enhances efficiency)	Positive (Brings desirable political neutrality)	Negative (Depersonalizes government)
Kind of merit system favored	Loosely implemented	Strong	None (Should be controlled by political elite)

Source: Adapted from Daniel J. Elazar, American Federalism: A View from the States, 2d ed. (New York: Thomas Y. Crowell, 1972), p. 100.

other parts of the country. It is therefore not surprising to learn that only about 47 percent of the cities in the South have civil service commissions, compared to the rest of the country where about 60 percent of all cities have such commissions.[18]

If, as Elazar maintains, the political culture is the crucial determinant in merit system viability, then the particular mechanics of merit system operations would seem to have little influence on the overall success or failure of the system. Studies in comparative administration have consistently found that "cultural differences will lead to differences in organizations even when identical technologies are used for the same purposes under identical conditions."[19] Consequently, jurisdictions with exactly the same legislative mandates, operating regulations, and staffing patterns will function one way within a moralistic political culture and in quite a different manner within an individualistic political culture. By extrapolating from what is known about the political culture of the environment, it is therefore possible to make reasonable predictions about the manner in which any civil service would function within that culture. Chicago is an excellent example. Its merit system, as might be culled from official documents, is the equal of many other jurisdictions. Historically Chicago is the city that pioneered modern position classification practices and many other personnel innovations. Yet, in practice, Chicago is well known to have one of the most patronage-ridden merit systems in the country, even though 97 percent of its municipal positions possess civil service status.[20]

Individuals have a tendency to judge the manifestations of political culture by their own biases. While it may be legalistically fair to judge a community or civil service system to be corrupt, this situation may or may not be actually deleterious to the community. Unfortunately, the civil service reform movement has so associated itself with morality in government that the real issues of governmental management have frequently been obscured. Righteous indignation is no substitute for empirical research. The reformers have never addressed themselves to the embarrassing success of immorality and corruption. It has long been observed in American literature and reality that "thrifty moral communities have a tendency to remain in the backwoods while a city like Chicago astonishes us with both its civic improvements and its political corruption."[21]

It has been widely observed that individuals tend to carry their cultural traits with them wherever they go. If such traits are not immediately recognizable, it is because they are latent, waiting for the appropriate conditions in which to surface.[22] For example, during the press coverage of the Watergate scandals, a variety of commentators noted that one of the conditions that led to the creation of a White House "dirty tricks" operation was the fact that President Nixon surrounded himself with advisers from Southern California, a region whose political style is "extremist, paranoid, and hortatory."[23] Within the Southern Californian political culture, the "attributes in a person to be admired are those which indicate his ability to enhance his position and expand his resources, not conserve his position and maintain his resources."[24] But just as individuals are ever evolving and subject to change, so too are the cultural values of the total community. Consequently, the cultural attributes of political jurisdictions

will, of necessity, always be ambiguous. "Static charac-
terizations of cities tend to understate the amount of internal conflict and potential for change which is present."[25]
The obviousness of such ongoing change is made evident by
the fact that "city government is vastly more honest, efficient, and democratic than it was a generation ago."[26]
This has been occasioned mainly by the evolution of the
community's political culture. The polyglot urban masses
of the early part of this century that were so easily manipulated by the machines and the bosses have tended to move
to the suburbs, if not literally then at least figuratively,
thereby adopting for their own "the political ideal of the
Anglo-Saxon Protestant middle-class political ethos."[27]
This discussion is necessarily simplistic; it must be recognized that ethnic roots are only one of a variety of factors that determine the political ethos of a community.[28]

   An understanding of political culture is the first
step toward a theoretical foundation for the design and
operation of public personnel systems. Without, at the
very least, a preliminary theoretical foundation, the design of public personnel systems will continue to be influenced more by the accident of short-term political and
administrative considerations than by the totality of
existing knowledge about organizational and political behavior. However, the study of political culture can tell
us only in the most general terms why some merit systems
tend to be more viable than others. A usable theory must
go farther than that. It must somehow provide for the optimal structural configuration of the system. It seems
reasonable to hypothesize that for each political culture
there are minimal support conditions without which a cred-
itable merit system cannot operate effectively. Once the
factors that lead to merit system vitality or debilitation
are extant, then the designers and reformers of civil service programs will have the kind of empirical evidence of
the validity of their proposals that should go a long way
in easing implementation. This seems to be a logical method
to establish the criteria upon which the design of public
personnel systems should be based.

   The basic research task in seeking a workable theory
would be to develop for each political culture measures of
efficacy for the constituent parts of the public personnel
system. By examining the political culture of any given
jurisdiction, it should be possible to measure the community's attitudes and dispositions toward merit system requirements. This "measure of political culture" could then
be taken into account in the design of any system. Juris-

dictions could avoid much institutionalized hypocrisy and malfeasance if they designed merit systems to complement rather than clash with their cultural environments. This is easier said than done. While one subculture is usually dominant, it is a rare jurisdiction that does not have another subculture influencing the community to a lesser extent. However, much of the country has been forced into the formal requirements of the moralistic political culture because it is the most rhetorically acceptable. To excise the hypocrisy and replace it with a civil service system that is appropriate for the community will be no easy task. It may well be impossible. How could civil service systems formally reflective of individualistic and traditionalistic political subcultures be reconciled with the conflicting national values of equal access and fair play? Besides, a legislative recognition of the practices engendered by these subcultures would undoubtedly violate a variety of constitutional provisions in addition to assorted federal statutes. Consequently, while the analysis of political culture may never be influential in the design of merit systems, it proves to be invaluable in explaining why such systems are ineffectual in certain cultural environments.

Political culture aside, there still is the major methodological problem of measurement. How is one system variable to be compared to another? What is the best organizational structure for the administration of a merit system? Is it the traditional independent civil service commission?[29] Or should the personnel department be under the jurisdictions' chief executive, as advocated by the Model Public Personnel Administration Law promulgated by the National Civil Service League?[30] The advantages and disadvantages of the various structural variations can be formulated into hypotheses and tested. Jurisdictions that have adopted a particular structural format can have their records compared for results before and after implementations, or adopting jurisdictions can have their programs compared to nonadopting jurisdictions of similar size and scope. An almost infinite variety of statistical measures can be realized to test the validity of a structural format. For example, we can measure whether an appointed director of personnel reporting directly to the chief executive allows the personnel department to be a more integrated member of the management team, generates an increase in patronage appointments, or provides for significant economies in operations.

While there is a wealth of information on public personnel systems, a major evaluation of such systems based upon empirical data does not exist. Until such data is available, the personnel operations of this country's jurisdictions will continue to be influenced more by emotions and happenstance than by logic and behavioral science.

NOTES

1. Carl Russell Fish, The Civil Service and the Patronage (Cambridge, Mass.: Harvard University Press, 1920), p. 42.

2. For example, see Everett G. Dillman, "The Impact of Culture on Management Practices," Public Personnel Review 31 (April 1970): 114-17; Virginia B. Ermer and John H. Strange, eds., Blacks and Bureaucracy: Readings in the Problems and Politics of Change (New York: Thomas Y. Crowell, 1972); Louis L. Knowles and Kenneth Prewitt, eds., Institutional Racism in America (Englewood Cliffs, N.J.: Prentice-Hall, Inc., 1969).

3. For example, see Felix A. Nigro, Modern Public Administration, 2d ed. (New York: Harper & Row, 1970), ch. 3; Joseph A. Litterer, The Analysis of Organizations, 2d ed. (New York: Wiley, 1973), ch. 12; Justin G. Longenecker, Principles of Management and Organizational Behavior (Columbus, Ohio: Charles E. Merrill, 1964), ch. 16.

4. Two exceptions to this are John Rehfuss, Public Administration as Political Process (New York: Charles Scribner's Sons, 1973), pp. 60-63; and Ira Sharkansky, Public Administration: Policy-Making in Government Agencies, 2d ed. (Chicago: Markam Publishing Co., 1972), pp. 197-200. Unfortunately, these texts go not much further in their examinations of political culture than to summarize the work of Daniel J. Elazar.

5. James Q. Wilson, Varieties of Police Behavior: The Management of Law & Order in Eight Communities (Cambridge, Mass.: Harvard University Press, 1968).

6. Ibid., ch. 5.

7. Melvin M. Belli, Review of The Finest Judges Money Can Buy, by Charles Ashman, in the New York Times Book Review, November 18, 1973, p. 42.

8. For example, see Robert A. Dahl, "The Science of Public Administration," in Claude E. Hawley and Ruth G. Weintraub, eds., Administrative Questions and Political Answers (Princeton, N.J.: D. Van Nostrand, 1966), p. 33. Dahl's article originally appeared in Public Administra-

135

tion Review 7, no. 1 (1947). Other examples are Dwight
Waldo, The Administrative State (New York: Ronald Press,
1948), p. 189; and James G. March and Herbert A. Simon,
Organizations (New York: Wiley, 1958), p. 68.

9. For methodological guides to the study of political culture, see Daniel J. Elazar, The Study of American
Political Culture. Working Kit no. 1, "Culture and the
Study of Political Culture"; Working Kit no. 2, "American
Political Culture and Its Subcultures" (Philadelphia:
Center for the Study of Federalism, Temple University,
1968); Andre Anthony Moore, Political Culture in Pennsylvania: An Empirical Analysis (Philadelphia: Center for
the Study of Federalism, Temple University, 1969).

10. Elazar notes that "the names given the three political subcultures are meant to be descriptive not eval-
uative. By the same token, the descriptions of the three
that follow are intended to be models or ideal types that
are not likely to be fully extant in the real world."
Daniel J. Elazar, American Federalism: A View from the
States, 2d ed. (New York: Thomas Y. Crowell, 1972), p.
93N.

11. Ibid., pp. 94-96.

12. Ibid., pp. 96-97, 99.

13. Ibid., pp. 99, 102. For an empirical confirma-
tion of the validity of Elazar's cultural trichotomy, see
Ira Sharkansky, "The Utility of Elazar's Political Culture: A Research Note," Polity 2 (Fall 1969): 66-83.

14. Daniel J. Elazar, Cities of the Prairie: The
Metropolitan Frontier and American Politics (New York:
Basic Books, 1970), p. 257. A similar definition can be
found in Donald J. Devine, The Political Culture of the
United States (Boston: Little, Brown & Co., 1972), pp.
14-18.

15. Elazar, Cities of the Prairie, p. 258.

16. For an article that dwells upon the reasons for
Minnesota's virtual lack of patronage and corruption, see
"Minnesota: A State That Works," Time, August 13, 1973,
pp. 24-35.

17. For highly readable accounts of patronage and cor-
ruption in Chicago, see Bill Gleason, Daley of Chicago:
The Man, the Mayor and the Limits of Conventional Politics
(New York: Simon & Schuster, 1970); Mike Royko, Boss:
Richard J. Daley of Chicago (New York: E. P. Dutton, 1971).

18. Winston W. Crouch, Guide for Modern Personnel Commissions (Chicago: International Personnel Management Association, 1973), p. 2. This has been historically true.
William C. Beyer made the same observation in the 1930s.

"Municipal Civil Service in the United States," in Carl J. Friedrich et al., Problems of the American Public Service (New York: McGraw-Hill, 1935), p. 86.

19. Joseph A. Litterer, The Analysis of Organizations, 2d ed. (New York: Wiley, 1973), p. 272.

20. Martin and Susan Tolchin, To the Victor: Political Patronage from the Clubhouse to the White House (New York: Vintage Books, 1971), p. 40. For a discussion of patronage techniques in Chicago, see pp. 33-45.

21. Thurman Arnold, The Symbols of Government (New Haven, Conn.: Yale University Press, 1935), p. 5.

22. For a discussion of latent culture, see Howard S. Becker and Blance Geer, "Latent Culture: A Note on the Theory of Latent Social Roles," Administrative Science Quarterly 5 (September 1960): 304-13.

23. Samuel C. Patterson, "The Political Culture of the American States," Journal of Politics 30 (February 1968): 203.

24. James Q. Wilson, "A Guide to Reagan Country: The Political Culture of Southern California," in Lewis Lipsitz, ed., The Confused Eagle: Division and Dilemma in American Politics (Boston: Allyn and Bacon, 1973), p. 132. This article originally appeared in Commentary 43 (May 1967): 37-45.

25. Robert R. Alford, Bureaucracy and Participation: Political Cultures in Four Wisconsin Cities (Chicago: Rand McNally, 1969), p. 35.

26. Edward C. Banfield and James Q. Wilson, City Politics (New York: Vintage Books, 1963), p. 149.

27. Ibid., p. 150.

28. Raymond E. Wolfinger and John Osgood Field, "Political Ethos and the Structure of City Government," American Political Science Review 60 (June 1966): 324-25.

29. For an analysis of the traditional role and functions of civil service commissions, see Winston W. Crouch, Guide for Modern Personnel Commissions.

30. For the pros and cons of the National Civil Service League's Model Law, see Jean J. Couturier, "The Model Public Personnel Administration Law: Two Views--Pro," Public Personnel Review 32 (October 1971): 202-09; and Harold E. Forbes, "The Model Public Personnel Administration Law: Two Views--Con," Public Personnel Review 32 (October 1971): 210-14.

CHAPTER

9

A NOTE OF OPTIMISM

Many critically important aspects of public personnel management have not been touched upon in this book. Such vital concerns as labor relations, manpower planning, affirmative action programs, and the whole panoply of traditional personnel functions have been dealt with only in passing. It must be recognized that some jurisdictions have had significant successes with upward mobility programs, training innovations, and overall organization development. It has never been the author's intent to minimize these praiseworthy achievements; on the contrary, by pointing out the natural inhibitors of such programs, these efforts should appear all the more remarkable. This book has been an attempt to discuss those features of the public personnel world that are most neglected in the generally available literature. Consequently, the end product of such an endeavor is very much reflective of the author's experience and biases. Some of the individuals who previewed the manuscript of this book observed how cynical the author is toward the machinations of the public personnel world. Any reasonable person would have to admit to cynicism toward the personnel operations of certain jurisdictions. But on the whole the author retains a cheerful optimism. This might seem an outrageous statement to those who have carefully read the preceding chapters. How can an author who has just delineated the boundaries of the netherworld of public personnel administration and has found many of its denizens to be in the same position as harlots suddenly assert his overall optimism on these matters? By looking at the proverbial forest instead of dwelling upon its legion of diseased trees, any reasonable analyst would also find substantial reason for long-term optimism. Two of the thorniest problems in public personnel management--equal employment opportunity and militant employee unions--can be used to test the validity of this hopeful outlook.

Perhaps the most outstanding single success of the American civil service has been the increasingly democratic nature of it. It has had to be pushed by the courts, by new legislation, and by rioting constituents, but it has moved. The situation has been so turned around from only a decade ago that the phenomenon of "reverse discrimination," whereby women and minorities are given preferential treatment, is analyzed in the liberal media with as much indignation and enthusiasm as the traditional modes of discrimination were lamented just a few years before. While racial and sexual discrimination was made illegal by a variety of legislative enactments, it remained for the courts to make equal employment opportunity a reality by requiring the examining process to be as nondiscriminatory as the formal hiring statutes.

The contents of many civil service examinations had been accused of being culturally biased in favor of certain segments of the population and/or irrelevant to the duties of the position for which the exam was being held. A variety of court rulings and empirical investigations have tended to uphold these accusations. The most significant of these is <u>Griggs</u> v. <u>Duke Power Company</u>, a case decided by the U.S. Supreme Court in 1971.[1] The court ruled that Title VII of the Civil Rights Act of 1964 "proscribes not only overt discrimination but also practices that are discriminatory in operation."[2] Thus, if employment practices operating to exclude minorities "cannot be shown to be related to job performance, the practice is prohibited."[3] The ruling also dealt a blow to restrictive credentialism when it stated that while diplomas and tests are useful, "Congress has mandated the commonsense proposition that they are not to become masters of reality."[4] In concluding, the court noted:

Nothing in the Act precludes the use of testing or measuring procedures; obviously they are useful. What Congress has forbidden is giving these devices and mechanisms controlling force unless they are demonstrably a reasonable measure of job performance. Congress has not commanded that the less qualified be preferred over the better qualified simply because of minority origins. Far from disparaging job qualifications as such, Con-

gress has made such qualifications the controlling
factor, so that race, religion, nationality, and
sex become irrelevant. What Congress has commanded
is that any tests used must measure the person for
the job and not the person in the abstract.[5]

In effect the Duke Power decision prohibited employers from using either a high school diploma or the passing
of a general intelligence examination as a precondition of
employment. Such practices were found to disqualify minorities at a higher rate than other applicants. The court's
attitude toward employment testing, while critical, is
likely to have very beneficial long-term results in that
personnel departments are now being pressured to provide
examining techniques that are valid and equitable to the
parent organization as well as to the potential employee
population. In order to comply with legal mandates, substantial resources will now have to be devoted to personnel
research. According to psychologist Floyd L. Ruch, "the
required investment in research will pay off not only by
satisfying government requirements, but also by increasing
the ability to identify in advance those employees who will
perform most effectively."[6]

The Duke Power decision is an excellent example of
how the Supreme Court acts to transform significant aspects
of American life. More than any other recent event in the
history of personnel administration, this decision will
radically influence the sophistication with which the profession is practiced. Employers, including government
jurisdictions at all levels, are now improving their examining processes under threat of court action or in antici-
pation of legal action. Alfred W. Blumrosen, formerly
Chief of Conciliations of the United States Equal Employment Opportunity Commission, maintains that the decision

is in the tradition of the great cases of constitutional and tort law which announce and apply
fundamental legal principles to the resolution of
basic and difficult problems of human relationships. The decision has poured decisive content
into a previously vacuous conception of human
rights. It shapes the statutory concept of "discrimination" in light of the social and economic
facts of our society. The decision restricts employers from translating the social and economic
subjugation of minorities into a denial of employment opportunity, and makes practical a prompt and

effective nationwide assault by both administrative agencies and the courts on patterns of discrimination.[7]

It has often been noted that in the United States, a country with twice as many lawyers per capita as any other, every important public issue becomes a legal problem. And so it is with the central question of civil service examinations: test validity. One might think that the validity of such exams could be appropriately determined by psychologists and other social scientists. But they can offer only professional opinions, whereas the opinion of a judge offers binding social legitimacy. While the courts may not be truly qualified to make such decisions, they provide the only available avenue for a face-saving compromise or defeat. The case of the Federal Service Entrance Examination illustrates this conditions. Candidates who had failed the FSEE filed suit against the U.S. Civil Service Commission alleging that the examination discriminated against minorities.[8] Each side brought forth psychologists to support their assertions.[9] The court accepted the defense's arguments that even though the exam is not work related, the abilities needed to pass the exam are those necessary and important for successful job performance.[10] Such a decision is in keeping with the Duke Power case, which did not mandate that all future examinations possess face validity, but simply insisted that they be demonstrable of "a reasonable measure of job performance." It can be anticipated that personnel research data obtained from position analysis questionnaires can aid in the "establishment of synthetically derived aptitude requirements of individual jobs."[11] The isolation of aptitude requirements of specific jobs would go a long way toward minimizing the need for situational validation.[12] When the historians of personnel operations look back at the past and coming decade, they no doubt will write that the Supreme Court markedly accelerated the pace of sophisticated aptitude examinations--so sophisticated and valid that such tests were able to withstand considerable litigation. Since conventional situational validations are exceedingly expensive, the personnel profession has little choice but to develop valid aptitude measures.

One would seem to have equal cause to be optimistic or pessimistic about the emergence of strong public employee unions. The extraordinary ability of unions to obtain fiscally crippling pay raises from their jurisdictions without yielding back any corresponding increases in productivity is certainly adequate cause for pessimism. However, the future of unions as vehicles to replace part of the merit system regalia and as a source of leadership in the fight for greater productivity is exceedingly hopeful. Militant public employee unions pose one overpowering problem that must be immediately addressed: Are they getting out of hand? Are their salaries and benefits becoming so great that the union members are no longer representative of the people they serve?

One of the major criticisms voiced during the Senate debate over the merits of the proposed Pendleton Act was that the creation of a career civil service would foster the development of a "fixed aristocratic class."[13] This had long been a concern of those opposed to reform.[14] After all, this was in fact the situation that existed through the Jackson administration.[15] While the spoils system had its obvious faults, it has generally been recognized by historians as responsible for the "democratization of administration on both the federal and state levels."[16] Since it was common knowledge that similar classes had long existed in Europe, serving as the bulwark of authoritarian rule, this concern was perhaps more than oppositional rhetoric or historical pettifoggery. While the reformers insisted that this would not, could not, be the case in this great democracy, there are many citizens who could argue rather persuasively today that this perhaps half-serious prediction of 1882 has, unfortunately, come true. To the extent that "aristocratic" implies that civil servants would have advantages generally denied to ordinary citizens, this dire prediction is already a fact in some of our largest jurisdictions. A cursory examination of salaries and pension benefits would support this contention. Salary surveys reveal with embarrassing frequency that government employees have salaries consistently higher than those for workers in identical geographical and occupational areas in the private sector. Many private firms say that "they can no longer compete with the government, and must adjust their pay rates upward whenever federal salaries are raised locally."[17] A survey of the city of Philadelphia's office workers by the Pennsylvania Economy League found that the salaries of city employees were 23.9 percent higher than for similar jobs in local industry.[18] While federal pay raises are frequently described as "catchups," personnel administrators in the private sector are saying that "we are the people who are doing the catching up now."[19] Executive salaries are a notable and shortsighted exception to this trend.

It is generally true that government jobs in large
jurisdictions offer significantly greater fringe benefits
than most private companies. While one could hardly claim
to justify aristocratic advantages on the basis of a few
more holidays or sick leave, government pension plans provide an example of the extraordinary advantage that public
employees enjoy at the expense of the common citizenry.
When pension plans for government employees began to emerge
during the second and third decades of this century, their
rationale was quite logical and simple. In the absence of
such programs, there was a tendency to retain on the payroll employees who were too old to perform their normal
duties. Since it is not a social tendency to reward many
years of faithful service with dismissal, employees frequently remained on the payroll as a matter of gratitude.
At a time when state, county, and municipal political machines almost always kept a variety of their stalwarts on
the payroll with "no show" jobs, this tactic was neither
unreasonable nor unparalleled. The drawbacks of retaining
decrepit employees notwithstanding, it was observed that it
was both kinder to the employee and cheaper for the taxpayer to provide pensions for those grown old in the public service. What started out as a measure to provide for
the old age of public servants has, a generation later,
turned into a rip-off of the public treasury.

The public is generally aware of pensions at half-pay
after 20 years for members of the armed services. What
was initially the compassionate concern of a grateful nation that its defenders not live in privation during their
old age has turned into a second income for that middle-
aged man working next to you. The obvious equity of providing generous annuities for those who put their lives on
the line for the nation is unquestioned until one learns
of Pentagon officers who retire and then reappear at the
Pentagon as civilian employees entitled to both their military pensions and civilian salaries. While there is nothing illegal about this so-called double dipping, it has
made a number of people question whether the public interest
is being adequately served.[20] Paralleling the pension program of the armed forces are the paramilitary service organizations, mainly police and fire departments. Again
the rationale for a retirement plan providing for half-pay
after 20 years of service is supplied by the inherent dangers and physical strains of such work. The dangers that
policemen and firemen face are certainly real. Nevertheless, it is the individual sanitation worker in New York
City who is more likely to be injured on the job. Admit-

tedly, however, few sanitation workers, in contrast to police and firemen, have occasion to die in the line of duty.

In some jurisdictions pension benefits are not simply
computed on the basis of one's salary, but on the basis
of one's total earnings during the previous year. Consequently, it is possible for an employee who worked a great
deal of overtime during his 20th year on the job to retire
with up to three-fourths of his base pay.[21] Such public
largess is no longer limited to military and paramilitary
services. With the advent of militant public employee
unions, an ever-increasing number of public servants in
all categories of employment are gaining the privilege of
retiring at half-pay after 20 years of service. But because of the method of computation, the general impression
of merely half-pay benefits is often misleading. For example, it is customary for retiring motormen of the New
York City Transit Authority to have overtime assigned to
them because pension benefits are computed on the basis of
the total earnings of the last year of service. "By as-
signing overtime to retiring motormen, rather than to more
junior employees, several million dollars in future pension
expenses were levied upon the city's public."[22]

In stark contrast to the situation in the larger jurisdictions, retirement provisions for public employees in
many smaller jurisdictions are grossly inadequate. But
the trends established by the larger jurisdictions are un-
mistakable. The United Auto Workers were delighted to have
achieved a 30-year retirement program at less than half-pay
in 1973,[23] when at the same time some large municipal jurisdictions had as a reality a 20-year retirement program
at half-pay or more for most, if not all, of their employees. All this has been achieved in just over a decade of
municipal union militancy. Such remarkable success was
due in large part to the "hidden" nature of pension benefits. Since such monies tend to come out of future bud-
gets, the incumbent executive can frequently bring himself
labor peace at the price of a fiscal headache for a future
incumbent of his office--not to mention taxpayer gouging.
Union members have been quite willing to accept "smaller"
salary increases in exchange for increased pension benefits.
They could hardly make a wiser financial investment. Probably the most disruptive municipal union strike action to
date occurred over the issue of pension benefits. When
the New York State Legislature failed to take action on a
pension bill for New York City's AFSCME Council 37,[24] some
members of that union sought to hasten the legislative
process by opening 27 of New York City's 39 movable

144

bridges.[25] The "trapping" of several hundred thousand
motorists in their cars for a number of hours had the opposite effect, and the legislature killed the bill for the
time being.

The generous pension benefits of public employees that
are now their right, or are rights they are likely to
achieve in the next few years, raises some serious philosophic and political questions for the polity. Should the
public tolerate financial benefits going to individuals,
ostensibly their servants, that are significantly greater
than what ordinary citizens can achieve within the economic
system? Is there any private industry that allows rank-
and-file employees to retire after 20 years with half-pay
or more for the rest of their lives? While the nation has
refused to adopt recommendations for a guaranteed annual
income without regard for work, many former and current
public servants already have or will have such a benefit
for as much as 20 years or more before what would ordinarily
be considered retirement age.

Why have public sector employees been able to gain
such privileges denied to the rest of society? The answer
lies in examining the political basis of their windfalls.
The military pension plans have been nursed along by an exceedingly strong lobbying effort on the part of past and
present military personnel, their families, and well-wishers.
Behind entreaties to the Congress has been the sacred symbol
of national security under whose aegis almost anything has
been justified.[26] The municipal unions have no symbol
anywhere near as potent as national security. So they have
resorted to bullying tactics and have been astonishingly
successful. They seem to be bullying their way into an
economic position where their financially related options
in life are significantly greater than the rest of the
community. One need not be a particularly astute political scientist to conclude that this is an unstable situation, not to be lightly tolerated by the populace. Assuming this trend continues unabated, it can only have one of
two long-term effects. It can be the harbinger of a trend
in the private sector whereby employees, increasingly more
concerned with the quality of their personal lives than
with salary increases, will seek and gain the option of an
early retirement similar to government practices. This
would either facilitate second careers or the leisurely
good life at the employee's option. But if the private
sector is unable or unwilling to offer benefits not too
far out of line with public sector benefits, it could
further enhance the alienation and cynicism that many citi-

zens already feel for their governments at all levels. It is of course impossible to predict the exact dangers that democratic forms of government face from loosening supports for their institutions and processes. But the present situation is obviously not healthy.

A study of municipal labor relations in New York City by Raymond D. Horton of Columbia University offers a detailed account of how this unhealthy situation came about.[27] While the lessons of New York are not wholly transferable to other jurisdictional contexts, Horton's weltansicht of municipal union-management relations as essentially a political struggle is a highly plausible explanation of why the leadership of municipal unions have been so remarkably successful in obtaining financial gains for their members during the last decade. Simply put, the union leaders have been the better politicians. Their acceptance of a militant posture directly followed the recognition that nontraditional forms of political behavior had been exceedingly productive for other interest groups in the city as well as the nation. Couple this with the fact that "management" is really a misnomer for the web of competitive political relationships existing among the various public officials involved with the collective bargaining process, and you have the basis for the rapid advances of municipal unions.

Horton views municipal labor relations as "a political contest between civil servants and public officials."[28] With both sides protecting mainly their own interests, the public has been the big loser while the unions have been the big winners. For example, during the four-year period ending in 1973, the actual salary earnings of New York City policemen and firemen increased 68.5 percent. These spectacular gains were realized largely because of Mayor Lindsay's efforts to depoliticize the labor relations process. By removing himself from the actual negotiations and installing intermediary impasse machinery, Mayor Lindsay abdicated a large portion of the authority over the public purse. The typical result was that whenever union leaders were unhappy about the wage offer they received from the mayor's representatives, they would directly or indirectly threaten a strike that would trigger the impasse machinery of "neutral" third parties who were quite willing to "split the difference." Why did these "neutrals" wind up giving away the store? Horton suggests three reasons: (1) it was not their responsibility to advocate the city's bargaining position; (2) they lacked the "muscle" of a mayor or his chief negotiator; (3) if neu-

trals wished to be selected for future employment in impasse
situations they could not afford to develop pro-management
reputations.

In adopting the policy of using presumably nonpoliti-
cal impasse machinery, the Lindsay administration "ceded
away authority and influence over municipal labor relations."[29] Of course, the justification for this approach
was labor peace. After a series of highly disruptive and
embarrassing strikes, peace was essential. But according
to Horton, Lindsay's peace was one of capitulation. The
result was higher taxes for the public and strong union
support for Mayor Lindsay in his campaign for re-election
to a second term. Aligning himself with those who feel
that New York City's municipal unions are too strong for
the public good, Horton advocates a repoliticization of
the negotiating process. Nor does Horton shy away from
his repoliticization stance when politics turns to conflict. "For public officials (and the public) always to
equate labor peace with the public interest represents a
kind of public death wish that ensures only that the municipal labor relations process will work better for organized
civil servants than for anyone else."[30] City officials
will not have a credible bargaining stance until the public
indicates a willingness to tolerate a few strikes long
enough to win them.

The preceding paragraphs have mainly dealt with the
more negative aspects of public employee unionism--nega-
tive at least from the viewpoint of the jurisdiction and
the citizenry. Nevertheless, it seems reasonable to hypothesize that this union cloud has a silver lining. Because
of the ever-expanding scope of negotiations, unions are
gradually whittling away at some of the most sacrosanct
practices of traditional merit systems. For example, the
extent to which they will make position classifications,
supervisory practices, and performance ratings more reflective of their will is open to considerable speculation.
But the inevitable by-product of this expanding union purview is the radical alteration of merit system concepts.
All parties must take care that straitjacket civil service
regulations are not simply negotiated away in exchange for
similarly constraining union policies. Once the unions
have gained all the financial benefits they reasonably
hope to attain, their leadership, like union leadership in
the private sector, will turn to the other most pressing
problem of their members--job satisfaction. Such a development will rebound to everyone's credit. Who could be opposed to the coupling of greater job satisfaction and in-

147

creased productivity? Such a massive redesign of governmental production with its necessarily attendant notions of
organizational power equalization can only be achieved with
the active cooperation of union leadership. A constella-
tion of factors, not the least of which will be pressure
from their constituents, will encourage union leadership
to assume a pivotal role in the redesign of jobs and the
enhancement, or at least the maintenance, of present levels
of productivity. In order to achieve the co-opting of
union leadership into the management process, public officials will have to yield or share a portion of their previously inviolate discretion; but this discretion is being
yielded bit by bit every year through the negotiating process anyway. It is better to create participative management by mutual consent with the goodwill and informality
that that entails than to see the development of adversary
relationships. There is a worldwide movement toward industrial democracy. Such participative management or power
equalization is founded upon highly respected and credit-
able behavioral research.[31] Voluminous case studies show
that as a concept it is equally operable in both capitalis-
tic and socialistic organizations. It has made significant
inroads in American industry in the last decade and will
be equally successful in governmental organizations once
the leadership of public employee unions come to realize
that the responsibilities that they bear toward their members is more than financial.

While public employee union leadership has not served
as a conspicuous example of probity and distinterested public service, the other side of the table, management in the
public sector, has seldom earned accolades for virtue.
All too frequently management is a perpetrator of what
Robert A. Dahl has called the "royal lie."[32] As the earlier discussion of the netherworld of public personnel administration has demonstrated, management frequently finds
it expedient to maintain two "truths" concerning personnel
actions--one for themselves and a more sanitized legally
correct one for public and employee consumption. Before
management can expect a cooperative and sympathetic attitude from employees and their representatives, they will
have to exhibit a greater degree of integrity about the
personnel process. For their part, public workers must
recognize the political nature of their employment milieu.
All the actors in the public personnel world must accept
their political fate--they cannot pretend either to themselves or to the public that they operate in a public sector counterpart to industrial personnel operations. The

political nature of public personnel management must be faced maturely. Just as the first step in arresting alcoholism is to have the alcoholic admit that he is an alcoholic and will always be an alcoholic even after he stops drinking, the first step toward putting public personnel operations on a more realistic footing is for public executives and union leaders alike to admit that public personnel operations are political processes even when traditional political considerations cease to dictate the minutia of personnel policy.

A first step toward achieving such a sense of reality is to make the public personnel netherworld inoperative. While it is easily agreed that its costs in terms of morale, efficiency, and criminality are too high, it will not be as easy for honest men of differing views to agree on how to supplant it. The last thing that is needed is traditional civil service reform in which the merit system is made tighter and tighter by further limiting the discretion of top management toward personnel matters. An environment must be created where managerial discretion is channeled toward decision making in support of the organizational mission rather than toward short-term political expediency. This seems to be a paradox. How is increased discretion over personnel decisions to be reconciled with the goal of directing executive actions toward nobler ends? One answer is to further institutionalize personnel processes. For example, it is the higher-level career system positions that are most subject to netherworld abuses. A little preventive action on the part of the personnel office could significantly change this situation. Well before top positions become vacant, lower-echelon career employees, who are possible candidates for such positions, could be identified and nominated as potential replacements. Managerial assessment centers are excellent devices for this purpose. The initiation of this kind of program would undoubtedly receive the widespread support of the career service, especially if the personnel department saw to it that an adequate amount of organizational publicity was associated with its implementation. While such a fanfare would augment the image of the jurisdiction as a good and fair place in which to work, more importantly, the existence of the program would make it all the more difficult for a political executive to ignore the program when the time came for another high-level appointment. The netherworld thrives in secrecy. If the decisional process is open to the scrutiny of the organization's employees as well as to the public, the political executive is almost

embarrassed into making a meritorious decision. His discretion remains intact; it is merely channeled through
existing institutions and processes. Since this kind of
institution building is informal in the sense that it is
not mandated by legislation, the political executive retains the option of appointing someone from outside the
career service. But such programs as the one outlined
above would tend to make it more likely that an individual
appointed from outside the career service would be at least
the equal of those available from the inside.

How does the cowering personnel officer dare to initiate such reforms? He bides his time and waits for the
appropriate moment. The whole history of American civil
service reform has been the story of the ebb and flow of
patronage quarrels, practices, and abuses. Reform tends
to be advocated by those out of power or leaving power in
order to deny its prerogative to the political opposition.
Even assuming the worst motives on the part of political
executives, personnel officials can institutionalize some
changes if their sense of timing is right. As one pro-
gresses up the scale from abject venality, ever greater
reforms are possible. This is essentially a test of the
will and political skill of the personnel officer. If he
declines to exhibit any will or exercise his political
skills, then he is no better than some of the scroundels
he may have had the occasion, if not the pleasure, to serve.

Public sector executives consistently complain about
being more hamstrung than helped by unwieldy and frequently,
in their opinion, unwarranted civil service procedures. In
fairness it must also be observed that political officeholders tend to complain about civil service restrictions
"regardless of the patronage they already control."[33]
But most public executives worth retaining already exercise
considerable influence over the personnel processes by subterfuge and stealth. Formally delegating to them powers
that they long ago acquired informally would hardly change
the balance of power between the personnel department, the
line managers, and the unions. And such a delegation would
not only eliminate one more pocket of administrative hypocrisy but would effect substantial savings as well. Instead
of establishing civil service systems that view top management and employees as adversaries or scoundrels before the
fact, cooperative systems that protect the interests of
the employees and the public without hamstringing its elective leadership should be designed. An important thrust
in this direction is the Model Personnel Administration Law
promulgated by the National Civil Service League. The or-

ganization that wrote the Pendleton Act, which created the present U.S. Civil Service Commission over 90 years ago, has come to the conclusion that civil service commissions as they typically operate are obsolete. The league now advocates placing the personnel function directly under a jurisdiction's chief executive with only a citizen's advisory board and an ombudsman to guard against the return of spoils. Yet all such proposals, no matter how circumspect, are likely to run into opposition from two powerful groups: the well-organized employee unions, ever concerned that an increase in the power and prerogatives of management will diminish their position; and less organized, less powerful, but equally articulate "good government" groups that are ever wary that an increase in managerial discretion will lead to a revitalized and runaway patronage program. The fears of both groups and the interests of effective managerial practices can surely be reconciled.

There are a variety of indicators that many of the worst abuses of the netherworld will decline somewhat in the coming years even if no formal reforms are undertaken. The maturing of public administration and public personnel administration as professional fields of endeavor will tend to increase the cosmopolitan outlook of its practitioners. The tremendous growth of academic programs in public administration has generated a lively concern with administrative ethics.[34] Even the American Society for Public Administration in association with the National Academy of Public Administration has recently published formal "Ethical Guidelines for Public Administrators."[35] All the various Watergate-related conspiracies have directed great attention to the problem of ethical behavior in the public service if only by serving as an object lesson on what happens if you get caught. In Robert Bolt's memorable play, A Man for All Seasons, the life of Sir Thomas More, the scholarly Chancellor of England who forfeited his life rather than accede to administrative expediency, is depicted. When pressed to deny his conscience on an administrative matter, More replies, "I believe, when statesmen forsake their own private conscience for the sake of their public duties . . . they lead their country by a short route to chaos."[36] Few of us are the stuff of martyrs. It is necessarily very difficult for a personnel operative among others to be guided by his conscience if this means putting his job on the line. But the development of rhetorically accepted ethical standards and the instilling of ethical concepts as a standard part of professional education for public administration should make it somewhat easier for personnelists to resist succumbing to harlotry in the future.

NOTES

1. Griggs v. Duke Power Co., 401 U.S. 424 (1971).
2. Ibid., p. 431.
3. Ibid.
4. Ibid., p. 433.
5. Ibid., p. 436.
6. Floyd L. Ruch, "The Impact on Employment Procedures of the Supreme Court Decision in the Duke Power Case," Personnel Journal 50 (October 1971): 783.
7. Alfred W. Blumrosen, "Strangers in Paradise: Griggs v. Duke Power Co. and the Concept of Employment Discrimination," Michigan Law Review 71 (November 1972): 62.
8. Douglas v. Hampton, 338 F. Supp. 18 (1972).
9. For the plaintiffs: Professor Philip Ash of the University of Illinois and Richard Barrett, a private consultant. For the CSC defense: the well-known Albert P. Maslow and William A. Gorham, the associate director of the CSC's Personnel Research and Development Center. Another study published by the Urban Institute found the FSEE "unfairly discriminatory to many black applicants." Robert Sadacca, The Validity and Discriminatory Impact of the Federal Service Entrance Examination (Washington, D.C.: Urban Institute, September 1971), p. 22.
10. On February 17, 1972, the U.S. District Court in Washington, D.C. denied the plaintiffs' motion for a preliminary injunction that would have halted the administration of the FSEE. The plaintiffs have filed an appeal but as of this writing there has been no final disposition.
11. Ernest J. McCormick, Paul R. Jeanneret, and Robert C. Mecham, "A Study of Job Characteristics and Job Dimensions as Based on the Position Analysis Questionnaire," Journal of Applied Psychology Monograph 56 (August 1972): 367.
12. Ibid., p. 347.
13. Carl Russell Fish, The Civil Service and the Patronage (New York: Russell & Russell, 1904, 1963), p. 220.
14. Leonard D. White, The Republican Era: A Study in Administrative History 1869-1901 (New York: Macmillan, 1958), p. 292.
15. Sidney H. Aronson, Status and Kinship in the Higher Civil Service (Cambridge, Mass.: Harvard University Press, 1964).
16. Carl N. Degler, Out of Our Past: The Forces that Shaped Modern America (New York: Harper Colophon Books, 1962), p. 141. Concurring with this notion is Arthur M. Schlesinger, Jr., The Age of Jackson (Boston: Little, Brown & Co., 1945), p. 46.

17. Mike Causey, "Secretarial Shortage Plagues U.S.,"
Washington Post, November 24, 1973, p. B9.

18. "How Do Salaries Compare?" Citizens Business
(Philadelphia: Pennsylvania Economy League, June 12, 1970),
p. 1.

19. Causey, "Secretarial Shortage Plagues U.S.," p. B9.

20. "Double Dipping in Federal Jobs Stirs up a Controversy," U.S. News & World Report, July 15, 1974, p. 45.

21. Sterling D. Spero and John M. Capozzola, The Ur-
ban Community and Its Unionized Bureaucracies: Pressure
Politics in Local Government Labor Relations (New York:
Dunellen, 1973), p. 225.

22. Raymond D. Horton, Municipal Labor Relations in
New York City: Lessons of the Lindsay-Wagner Years (New
York: Praeger, 1973), p. 100.

23. New York Times, September 23, 1973, p. E3.

24. The New York State Legislature must approve all
New York City pension programs before they can become law.
The city had already agreed to the union's demands before
the strike.

25. This was the famous "drawbridge" strike. For accounts, see the New York Times, June 8, 9, 10, 1973.

26. The unfailing logic of the national security rationale when it is applied to pension benefits is that
good men will not muster to the colors unless they are assured of generous pensions at an early age.

27. Horton, Municipal Labor Relations in New York City.

28. Ibid., p. 45.

29. Ibid., p. 76.

30. Ibid., p. 131.

31. The best introductory surveys of this movement
and the research that supports its intellectual foundations
are Paul Blumberg, Industrial Democracy: The Sociology of
Participation (New York: Schocken Books, 1968); and David
Jenkins, Job Power: Blue and White Collar Democracy (Baltimore: Penguin Books, 1974).

32. Robert A. Dahl, After the Revolution? Authority
in a Good Society (New Haven, Conn.: Yale University
Press, 1970), p. 10.

33. Martin and Susan Tolchin, To the Victor: Political Patronage from the Clubhouse to the White House (New
York: Vintage Books, 1971), p. 72.

34. The best critique of this is Eugene P. Dvorin and
Robert H. Simmons, From Amoral to Humane Bureaucracy (New
York: Harper & Row, 1972).

35. George A. Graham, "Ethical Guidelines for Public
Administrators: Observations on Rules of the Game," Pub-

lic Administration Review 34 (January-February 1974):
90-92. The guidelines are subject to revision.

36. Robert Bolt, A Man for All Seasons (New York:
Random House, 1962), p. 22. When Robert Mardian, an assistant attorney general, complained to a reporter from the
Wall Street Journal that we are getting more people in
government who feel they should be ruled by a sense of
conscience "rather than what the bureaucracy expects of
them," Senator Adlai Stevenson used the occasion to go on
record and say that "I would prefer, and I believe the
American people would prefer, that our public servants be
guided by conscience." Nation, April 17, 1972, p. 485.
Two years later Robert Mardian, along with Haldeman, Ehr-
lichman, Mitchell, et al., was indicted on charges concerning the Watergate cover-up conspiracy.

BOOKS

Adrian, Charles R., and Charles Press. Governing Urban America. 4th ed. New York: McGraw-Hill, 1972.

Alford, Robert R. Bureaucracy and Participation: Political Cultures in Four Wisconsin Cities. Chicago: Rand McNally, 1969.

Appleby, Paul. Policy and Administration. University: University of Alabama Press, 1949.

Arendt, Hannah. Crises of the Republic. New York: Harcourt, Brace, Jovanovich, 1972.

Arnold, Thurman W. The Symbols of Government. New Haven, Conn.: Yale University Press, 1935.

Aronson, Sidney H. Status and Kinship in the Higher Civil Service. Cambridge, Mass.: Harvard University Press, 1964.

Ashman, Charles R. The Finest Judges Money Can Buy. Los Angeles: Nash Publishing Corp., 1973.

Banfield, Edward C., and James Q. Wilson. City Politics. New York: Vintage Books, 1963.

Barnard, Chester I. The Functions of the Executive. 30th anniversary ed. Cambridge, Mass.: Harvard University Press, 1968.

Beard, Charles. American City Government. New York: The Century Co., 1912.

Becker, Theodore L., and Vernon G. Murray, eds. Government Lawlessness in America. New York: Oxford University Press, 1971.

Bell, Daniel. Work and Its Discontents: The Cult of Efficiency in America. Boston: Beacon Press, 1956.

Bennis, Warren G., et al. *Personnel Dialogue for the Seventies*. Chicago: Public Personnel Association, Personnel Report no. 712, 1971.

Benveniste, Guy. *The Politics of Expertise*. Berkeley, Calif.: The Glendessary Press, 1972.

Blumberg, Paul. *Industrial Democracy: The Sociology of Participation*. New York: Schocken Books, 1968.

Bolt, Robert. *A Man for All Seasons*. New York: Random House, 1962.

Boyer, Brian D. *Cities Destroyed for Cash: The FHA Scandal at HUD*. Chicago: Follett Publishing Co., 1973.

Bruere, Henry. *New City Government*. New York: D. Appleton, 1913.

Bryce, James. *The American Commonwealth*. New ed. New York: Macmillan, 1917.

Caiden, Gerald E. *The Dynamics of Public Administration: Guidelines to Current Transformations in Theory and Practice*. New York: Holt, Rinehart and Winston, 1971.

Carman, Harry J., and Reinhard H. Luthin. *Lincoln and the Patronage*. New York: Columbia University Press, 1943.

Carpenter, William Seal. *The Unfinished Business of Civil Service Reform*. Princeton, N.J.: Princeton University Press, 1952.

Charlesworth, James C. *Governmental Administration*. New York: Harper & Bros., 1951.

Cobb, Roger W., and Charles D. Elder. *Participation in American Politics: The Dynamics of Agenda-Building*. Boston: Allyn and Bacon, 1972.

Cooke, Charles. *Biography of an Ideal: The Diamond Anniversary History of the Federal Civil Service*. Washington, D.C.: U.S. Government Printing Office, 1959.

Cressey, Donald R. *Theft of the Nation: The Structure and Operations of Organized Crime in America*. New York: Harper Colophon Books, 1969.

156

Croly, Herbert. The Promise of American Life. New York: Macmillan, 1909.

Crouch, Winston W. Guide for Modern Personnel Commissions. Chicago: International Personnel Management Association, 1973.

Dahl, Robert A. After the Revolution? Authority in a Good Society. New Haven, Conn.: Yale University Press, 1970.

Dalby, Michael T., and Michael S. Werthman, eds. Bureaucracy in Historical Perspective. Glenview, Ill.: Scott, Foresman and Co., 1971.

Davis, James C. Human Nature in Politics: The Dynamics of Political Behavior. New York: Wiley, 1963.

Davis, Keith. Human Behavior at Work: Human Relations and Organizational Behavior. 4th ed. New York: McGraw-Hill, 1972.

Degler, Carl N. Out of Our Past: The Forces that Shaped Modern America. New York: Harper Colophon Books, 1962.

Devine, Donald J. The Political Culture of the United States. Boston: Little, Brown & Co., 1972.

Devlin, Thomas C. Municipal Reform in the United States. New York: G. P. Putnam's Sons, 1896.

Dimock, Marshall E., and Gladys O. Dimock. Public Administration. 4th ed. New York: Holt, Rinehart and Winston, 1969.

Donald, David. Lincoln Reconsidered. New York: Knopf, 1959.

Dowling, William F., Jr., and Leonard R. Sayles. How Managers Motivate: The Imperatives of Supervision. New York: McGraw-Hill, 1971.

Duncan, Hugh D. Communication and Social Order. New York: Bedminster Press, 1962.

Dvorin, Eugene P., and Robert H. Simmons. From Amoral to Human Bureaucracy. New York: Canfield Press, Harper & Row, 1972.

Eaton, Dorman B. Civil Service in Great Britain. New York: Harper & Bros., 1880.

Easton, David. The Political System: An Inquiry into the State of Political Science. 2d ed. New York: Knopf, 1971.

Edelman, Murray. The Symbolic Uses of Politics. Urbana: University of Illinois Press, 1967.

Elazar, Daniel J. American Federalism: A View from the States. 2d ed. New York: Thomas Y. Crowell, 1972.

_____. Cities of the Prairie: The Metropolitan Frontier and American Politics. New York: Basic Books, 1970.

_____. The Study of American Political Culture. Working Kit no. 1, "Culture and the Study of Political Culture"; Working Kit no. 2, "American Political Culture and Its Subcultures." Philadelphia: Center for the Study of Federalism, Temple University, 1968.

Ermer, Virginia B., and John H. Strange, eds. Blacks and Bureaucracy: Readings in the Problems and Politics of Change. New York: Thomas Y. Crowell, 1972.

Etzioni, Amitai. Modern Organizations. Englewood Cliffs, N.J.: Prentice-Hall, 1964.

Fesler, James W., ed. The 50 States and Their Local Governments. New York: Knopf, 1967.

Fish, Carl Russell. The Civil Service and the Patronage. New York: Russell & Russell, 1904, 1963.

Fitzpatrick, Edward A., ed. Experts in City Government. New York: D. Appleton, 1919.

Flory, Charles D., and R. Alec Mackenzie. The Credibility Gap in Management. New York: Van Nostrand Reinhold Co., 1971.

Ford, Robert N. *Motivation Through the Work Itself*. New York: American Management Association, 1969.

Foulkes, Fred K. *Creating More Meaningful Work*. New York: American Management Association, 1969.

French, Wendell L., and Cecil H. Bell, Jr. *Organization Development: Behavioral Science Interventions for Organization Improvement*. Englewood Cliffs, N.J.: Prentice-Hall, 1973.

French, Wendell L., and Don Hellriegel, eds. *Personnel Management and Organization Development: Fields in Transition*. Boston: Houghton Mifflin Co., 1971.

Friedrich, Carl J. *The Pathology of Politics*. New York: Harper & Row, 1972.

Friedrich, Carl J., et al. *Problems of the American Public Service*. New York: McGraw Hill, 1935.

Geisler, Edwin B. *Manpower Planning: An Emerging Staff Function*. New York: American Management Association, 1967.

George, Claude S., Jr. *The History of Management Thought*. 2d ed. Englewood Cliffs, N.J.: Prentice-Hall, 1972.

Gerth, H. H., and C. Wright Mills. *From Max Weber: Essays in Sociology*. New York: Oxford University Press, 1946.

Gladden, E. N. *Civil Services of the United Kingdom*. New York: Augustus M. Kelley, 1967.

_____. *A History of Public Administration*. London: Frank Cass, 1972.

Gleason, Bill. *Daley of Chicago: The Man, the Mayor and the Limits of Conventional Politics*. New York: Simon & Schuster, 1970.

Goffman, Erving. *Relations in Public: Microstudies of the Public Order*. New York: Harper Colophon Books, 1972.

159

Goldman, Eric F. _Rendezvous with Destiny: A History of Modern American Reform_. New York: Knopf, 1965.

Golembiewski, Robert T., and Michael Cohen, eds. _People in Public Services: A Reader in Public Personnel Administration_. Itasca, Ill.: F. E. Peacock Publishers, 1970.

Golembiewski, Robert T., Frank Gibson, and Geoffrey Cornog, eds. _Public Administration: Readings in Institutions, Processes, Behavior_. 2d ed. Chicago: Rand McNally, 1972.

Gooding, Judson. _The Job Revolution_. New York: Walker, 1972.

Grant, Daniel R., and H. C. Nixon. _State and Local Government in America_. 2d ed. Boston: Allyn and Bacon, 1968.

Greenstein, Fred I. _The American Party System and the American People_. Englewood Cliffs, N.J.: Prentice-Hall, 1963.

Hanford, A. Chester. _Problems in Municipal Government_. Chicago: A. W. Shaw, 1926.

Harvey, Donald R. _The Civil Service Commission_. New York: Praeger, 1970.

Hawley, Claude E., and Ruth C. Weintraub, eds. _Administrative Questions and Political Answers_. Princeton, N.J.: D. Van Nostrand, 1966.

Herzberg, Frederick. _Work and the Nature of Man_. Cleveland, Ohio: World Publishing Company, 1966.

_____, Bernard Mausner, and Barbara B. Snyderman. _The Motivation to Work_. New York: Wiley, 1959.

Hicks, Herbert G., ed. _Management, Organizations and Human Resources: Selected Readings_. New York: McGraw-Hill, 1972.

_____. _The Management of Organizations: A Systems and Human Resources Approach_. 2d ed. New York: McGraw-Hill, 1972.

Hodge, Billy J., and Herbert J. Johnson. _Management and Organizational Behavior: A Multidimensional Approach_. New York: Wiley, 1970.

Hofstadter, Richard. _The Age of Reform_. New York: Vintage Books, 1955.

_____. _The American Political Tradition_. New York: Vintage Books, 1948.

Hoogenboom, Ari. _Outlawing the Spoils: A History of the Civil Service Reform Movement: 1865-1883_. Urbana: University of Illinois Press, 1961.

Hoover, Herbert C. _The Memoirs of Herbert Hoover: The Cabinet and the Presidency, 1920-1933_. New York: Macmillan, 1952.

Horton, Raymond D. _Municipal Labor Relations in New York City: Lessons of the Lindsay-Wagner Years_. New York: Praeger, 1973.

Howton, F. William. _Functionaries_. Chicago: Quadrangle Books, 1969.

Hyneman, Charles S. _Bureaucracy in a Democracy_. New York: Harper & Bros., 1950.

International City Manager's Association. _Municipal Personnel Administration_. 6th ed. Chicago: ICMA, 1960.

Jay, Anthony. _Corporation Man_. New York: Random House, 1971.

_____. _Management and Machiavelli: An Inquiry into the Politics of Corporate Life_. New York: Holt, Rinehart and Winston, 1967.

Jenkins, David. _Job Power: Blue and White Collar Democracy_. Baltimore: Penguin Books, 1974.

Josephson, Matthew. _The Politicos: 1865-1896_. New York: Harcourt, Brace & Company, 1938.

Kahler, Gerald E., and Alton C. Johnson. _The Development of Personnel Administration, 1923-1945_. Madison: University of Wisconsin, Graduate School of Business,

Bureau of Business Research and Service, Monograph no. 3, January 1971.

Kammerer, Gladys M. Impact of War on Federal Personnel Administration, 1939-1945. Lexington: University of Kentucky Press, 1951.

Katz, Daniel, and Robert L. Kahn. The Social Psychology of Organizations. New York: Wiley, 1966.

Kaufman, Herbert. Administrative Feedback in Monitoring Subordinates' Behavior. Washington, D.C.: Brookings Institution, 1973.

Knowles, Louis L., and Kenneth Prewitt, eds. Institutional Racism in America. Englewood Cliffs, N.J.: Prentice-Hall, Inc., 1969.

Koenig, Louis W. The Chief Executive. Rev. ed. New York: Harcourt, Brace & World, 1968.

Kramer, Leo. Labor's Paradox: The American Federation of State, County, and Municipal Employees AFL-CIO. New York: Wiley, 1962.

Krause, Elliott A. The Sociology of Occupations. Boston: Little, Brown & Co., 1971.

Landsberger, Henry A. Hawthorne Revisited. Ithaca, N.Y.: Cornell University Press, 1958.

Levinson, Harry. The Exceptional Executive: A Psychological Conception. Cambridge, Mass.: Harvard University Press, 1968.

Ling, Cyril Curtis. The Management of Personnel Relations: History and Origins. Homewood, Ill.: Richard D. Irwin, 1965.

Lipsitz, Lewis, ed. The Confused Eagle: Division and Dilemma in American Politics. Boston: Allyn and Bacon, 1973.

Litterer, Joseph A. The Analysis of Organizations. 2d ed. New York: Wiley, 1973.

Longenecker, Justin G. <u>Principles of Management and Organizational Behavior</u>. Columbus, Ohio: Charles E. Merrill, 1964.

Loory, Stuart H. <u>Defeated: Inside America's Military Machine</u>. New York: Random House, 1973.

Lowi, Theodore J. <u>At the Pleasure of the Mayor: Patronage and Power in New York City, 1898-1958</u>. New York: The Free Press, 1964.

Machiavelli, Niccolo. <u>The Prince</u> and <u>The Discourses</u>. New York: Modern Library, 1950.

Macy, John W., Jr. <u>Public Service: The Human Side of Government</u>. New York: Harper & Row, 1971.

Maher, John R., ed. <u>New Perspectives in Job Enrichment</u>. New York: Van Nostrand Reinhold Co., 1971.

Mailer, Norman. <u>Miami and the Siege of Chicago</u>. New York: Signet, 1968.

Mailick, Sidney, and Edward H. Van Ness, eds. <u>Concepts and Issues in Administrative Behavior</u>. Englewood Cliffs, N.J.: Prentice-Hall, 1962.

Mainzer, Lewis C. <u>Political Bureaucracy</u>. Glenview, Ill.: Scott, Foresman & Co., 1973.

March, James G., and Herbert A. Simon. <u>Organizations</u>. New York: Wiley, 1958.

Marx, Fritz Morstein. <u>The Administrative State: An Introduction to Bureaucracy</u>. Chicago: University of Chicago Press, 1957.

McBain, Howard Lee. <u>DeWitt Clinton and the Origin of the Spoils System in New York</u>. New York: AMS Press, Inc., 1967.

McCurdy, Howard E. <u>Public Administration: A Bibliography</u>. Washington, D.C.: College of Public Affairs, American University, 1972.

McFarland, Dalton E. <u>Cooperation and Conflict in Personnel Administration</u>. New York: American Foundation for Management Research, 1962.

163

McGregor, Douglas. _The Human Side of Enterprise_. New
   York: McGraw-Hill, 1960.

Meriam, Lewis. _Personnel Administration in the Federal
   Government_. Washington, D.C.: Brookings Institution,
   1937.

_____. _Public Personnel Problems: From the Standpoint
   of the Operating Officer_. Washington, D.C.: Brookings Institution, 1938.

Merton, Robert K. _Social Theory and Social Structure_.
   Rev. ed. Glencoe, Ill.: The Free Press of Glencoe,
   1957.

Milgram, Stanley. _Obedience to Authority: An Experimental
   View_. New York: Harper & Row, 1973.

Milton, Charles R. _Ethics and Expediency in Personnel Management: A Critical History of Personnel Philosophy_.
   Columbia: University of South Carolina Press, 1970.

Mollenhoff, Clark R. _Strike Force: Organized Crime and
   the Government_. Englewood Cliffs, N.J.: Prentice-
   Hall, 1972.

Moore, Andre Anthony. _Political Culture in Pennsylvania:
   An Empirical Analysis_. Philadelphia: Center for the
   Study of Federalism, Temple University, 1969.

Morison, Samuel Eliot. _The Oxford History of the American
   People_. New York: Oxford University Press, 1965.

Mosher, Frederick C. _Democracy and the Public Service_.
   New York: Oxford University Press, 1968.

Mosher, William E., and J. Donald Kingsley. _Public Personnel Administration_. New York: Harper & Bros.,
   1936.

Municipal Manpower Commission. _Governmental Manpower for
   Tomorrow's Cities_. New York: McGraw-Hill, 1962.

Myers, M. Scott. _Every Employee a Manager_. New York:
   McGraw-Hill, 1970.

Nader, Ralph, Peter J. Petkas, and Kate Blackwell, eds. _Whistle Blowing: The Report of the Conference on Professional Responsibility_. New York: Grossman, 1972.

Niederhoffer, Arthur. _Behind the Shield: The Police in Urban Society_. Garden City, N.Y.: Doubleday Anchor, 1969.

Nigro, Felix A. _Modern Public Administration_. 2d ed. New York: Harper & Row, 1970.

Odegard, Holtan P. _The Politics of Truth: Toward Reconstruction in Democracy_. University: University of Alabama Press, 1971.

Odiorne, George S. _Personnel Administration by Objectives_. Homewood, Ill.: Richard D. Irwin, 1971.

Ogden, C. K., and I. A. Richards, eds. _The Meaning of Meaning: A Study of the Influence of Language upon Thought and of the Science of Symbolism_. New York Harcourt, Brace, 1945.

Patten, Thomas H., Jr. _Manpower Planning and the Development of Human Resources_. New York: Wiley, 1971.

Paul, W. J., and K. B. Robertson. _Job Enrichment and Employee Motivation_. London: Gower Press, 1970.

Peskin, Dean B. _The Doomsday Job: The Behavioral Anatomy of Turnover_. New York: AMACOM, 1973.

Peter, Laurence J., and Raymond Hull. _The Peter Principle_. New York: Bantam Books, 1970.

Peters, Charles, and Taylor Branch, eds. _Whistle Blowing: Dissent in the Public Interest_. New York: Praeger, 1972.

Pfiffner, John M. _Municipal Administration_. New York: Ronald Press, 1940.

_____. _Public Administration_. New York: Ronald Press, 1935.

Pfiffner, John M., and Marshall Fells. _The Supervision of Personnel: Human Relations in the Management of Men_. 3d ed. Englewood Cliffs, N.J.: Prentice-Hall, 1964.

Pfiffner, John M., and Frank P. Sherwood. *Administrative Organization*. Englewood Cliffs, N.J.: Prentice-Hall, 1960.

Pigors, Paul, and Charles A. Myers. *Personnel Administration: A Point of View and a Method*. New York: McGraw-Hill, 1969.

Popper, Frank. *The President's Commissions*. New York: Twentieth Century Fund, 1970.

Powell, Norman J. *Personnel Administration in Government*. Englewood Cliffs, N.J.: Prentice-Hall, 1956.

Rehfuss, John. *Public Administration as Political Process*. New York: Charles Scribner's Sons, 1973.

Richardson, James F., ed. *The American City: Historical Studies*. Waltham, Mass.: Xerox College Publishing, 1972.

Ritzer, George, and Harrison M. Trice. *An Occupation in Conflict: A Study of the Personnel Manager*. Ithaca: New York State School of Industrial and Labor Relations, Cornell University, 1969.

Roethlisberger, F. J., and William J. Dickson. *Management and the Worker*. Cambridge, Mass.: Harvard University Press, 1939.

Rosenberg, Hans. *Bureaucracy, Aristocracy and Autocracy: The Prussian Experience 1660-1815*. Cambridge, Mass.: Harvard University Press, 1958.

Royko, Mike. *Boss: Richard J. Daley of Chicago*. New York: E. P. Dutton, 1971.

Sadacca, Robert. *The Validity and Discriminatory Impact of the Federal Service Entrance Examination*. Washington, D.C.: Urban Institute, September 1971.

Sayre, Wallace S., and Herbert Kaufman. *Governing New York City: Politics in the Metropolis*. New York: W. W. Norton, 1965.

Schattschneider, E. E. *Party Government*. New York: Farrar and Rinehart, 1942.

_____. The Semi-Sovereign People: A Realist's View of Democracy in America. New York: Holt, Rinehart and Winston, 1960.

Schinagl, Mary S. History of Efficiency Ratings in the Federal Government. New York: Bookman Associates, 1966.

Schlesinger, Arthur M., Jr. The Age of Jackson. Boston: Little, Brown, & Co., 1945.

Schoderbek, Peter P., and William E. Reif. Job Enlargement: Key to Improved Performance. Ann Arbor: Bureau of Industrial Relations, University of Michigan, 1969.

Seidman, Harold. Politics, Position, & Power: The Dynamics of Federal Organization. New York: Oxford University Press, 1970.

Shafritz, Jay M. Position Classification: A Behavioral Analysis for the Public Service. New York: Praeger, 1973.

Sharkansky, Ira. Public Administration: Policy-Making in Government Agencies. 2d ed. Chicago: Markam Publishing Co., 1972.

Skidmore, Max J. Medicare and the American Rhetoric of Reconciliation. University: University of Alabama Press, 1970.

Smith, Darrell Hevenor. The United States Civil Service Commission: Its History, Activities and Organization. Baltimore: The Johns Hopkins Press, 1928.

Snider, Clyde F. American State and Local Government. 2d ed. New York: Appleton-Century-Crofts, 1965.

Spero, Sterling D., and John M. Capozzola. The Urban Community and Its Unionized Bureaucracies: Pressure Politics in Local Government Labor Relations. New York: Dunellen, 1973.

Stahl, O. Glenn. Public Personnel Administration. 6th ed. New York: Harper & Row, 1971.

Stainer, Gareth. _Manpower Planning: The Management of Human Resources_. London: Heinemann, 1971.

Stave, Bruce M., ed. _Urban Bosses, Machines, and Progressive Reformers_. Lexington, Mass.: D. C. Heath, 1972.

Steffens, Lincoln. _The Autobiography of Lincoln Steffens_. Chautauqua, N.Y.: Chautauqua Press, 1931.

Stewart, Frank Mann. _The National Civil Service Reform League: History, Activities, and Problems_. Austin: University of Texas, 1929.

Thompson, Victor A. _Modern Organization_. New York: Knopf, 1969.

Tolchin, Martin, and Susan Tolchin. _To the Victor: Political Patronage from the Clubhouse to the White House_. New York: Vintage Books, 1971.

Townsend, Robert. _Up the Organization: How to Stop the Corporation from Stifling People and Strangling Profits_. Greenwich, Conn.: Fawcett, 1970.

Vaughn, Robert. _The Spoiled System_. Washington, D.C.: Public Interest Research Group, 1972.

Van Riper, Paul P. _History of the United States Civil Service_. Evanston, Ill.: Row, Peterson & Co., 1958.

Waldo, Dwight. _The Administrative State_. New York: Ronald Press, 1948.

Waldo, Dwight, ed. _Ideas and Issues in Public Administration_. New York: McGraw-Hill, 1953.

Ward, John William. _Andrew Jackson: Symbol for an Age_. New York: Oxford University Press, 1962.

Weinstein, James. _The Corporate Ideal in the Liberal State in 1900-1918_. Boston: Beacon Press, 1968.

White, Leonard D. _The Federalists_. New York: Macmillan, 1948.

_____. _Introduction to the Study of Public Administration_. 4th ed. New York: Macmillan, 1955.

_____. The Jacksonians. New York: Macmillan, 1954.

_____. The Jeffersonians. New York: Macmillan, 1951.

_____. The Republican Era: A Study in Administrative
History: 1869-1901. New York: The Free Press, 1958.

_____. Trends in Public Administration. New York: Mc-
Graw-Hill, 1933.

White, Morton, and Lucia White. The Intellectual Versus
the City: From Thomas Jefferson to Frank Lloyd Wright.
Cambridge, Mass.: Harvard University Press, 1962.

Wilson, James Q. Varieties of Police Behavior: The Management of Law and Order in Eight Communities. Cambridge, Mass.: Harvard University Press, 1968.

Wikstrom, Walter S. Manpower Planning: Evolving Systems.
New York: The Conference Board, 1971.

Wise, David. The Politics of Lying: Government, Deception,
Secrecy, and Power. New York: Random House, 1973.

Woll, Peter, ed. Public Administration and Policy. New
York: Harper & Row, 1966.

Wren, Daniel A. The Evolution of Management Thought. New
York: Ronald Press, 1972.

PERIODICALS

Auerbach, Arnold J. "Confrontation and Administrative
Response." Public Administration Review, vol. 29
(November-December 1969).

Bachrach, Peter, and Morton S. Baratz. "Decisions and Nondecisions: An Analytical Framework." American Political Science Review, vol. 57 (December 1963).

Baker, Walter. "Management by Objectives: A Philosophy
and Style of Management for the Public Sector." Canadian Public Administration, vol. 12 (Fall 1969).

Becker, Howard S., and Blance Geer. "Latent Culture: A
Note on the Theory of Latent Social Roles." Administrative Science Quarterly, vol. 5 (September 1960).

Blumrosen, Alfred W. "Strangers in Paradise: Griggs v. Duke Power Co. and the Concept of Employment Discrimination." Michigan Law Review, vol. 71 (November 1972).

Brady, Rodney H. "MGO Goes to Work in the Public Sector." Harvard Business Review, vol. 51 (March-April 1973).

Caiden, Gerald E. "Public Personnel Administration in the Doldrums?" Public Personnel Review, vol. 32 (January 1971).

Calhoon, Richard P. "Niccolo Machiavelli and the Twentieth Century Administrator." Academy of Management Journal, vol. 12 (June 1969).

Cobb, Roger W., and Charles D. Elder. "The Political Uses of Symbolism." American Politics Quarterly, vol. 1 (July 1973).

Cochran, Andrew H. "Management Tigers and Pussycats." Personnel Journal, vol. 50 (December 1971).

Congressional Quarterly, January 3, 1969.

Couturier, Jean J. "Civil Service Reform--1970s Style." Good Government, vol. 90 (Summer 1973).

_____. "The Model Public Personnel Administration Law: Two Views--Pro." Public Personnel Review, vol. 32 (October 1971).

Derthick, Martha. "On Commissionship-Presidential Variety." Public Policy, vol. 19 (Fall 1971).

Dillman, Everett G. "The Impact of Culture on Management Practices." Public Personnel Review, vol. 31 (April 1970).

DiNunzio, A., and Nancy Hall. "Manning Tomorrow's Cities: In Search of Professionals." Nation's Cities, vol. 11 (June 1973).

Domm, Donald R., and James E. Stafford. "Personnel: Behind the Times." Personnel Journal, vol. 49 (July 1970).

Drucker, Peter F. "The Sickness of Government." Public Interest, vol. 14 (Winter 1969).

Eriksson, Erik M. "The Federal Civil Service Under President Jackson." <u>Mississippi Valley Historical Review</u>, vol. 13 (March 1927).

Etzioni, Amitai. "Two Approaches to Organizational Analysis: A Critique and a Suggestion." <u>Administrative Science Quarterly</u>, vol. 5 (September 1960).

Eulau, Heinz. "A Note on the Discipline: Quo Vadimus?" <u>P.S.: Newsletter of the American Political Science Association</u>, Winter 1969.

Famiglietti, Len. "Personnel Officers Subject of Review." <u>Federal Times</u>, January 17, 1973.

Forbes, Harold E. "The Model Public Personnel Administration Law: Two Views--Con." <u>Public Personnel Review</u>, vol. 32 (October 1971).

Ford, Robert N. "Job Enrichment Lessons from AT&T." <u>Harvard Business Review</u>, vol. 51 (January-February 1973).

"Future Trends in Public Administration--Predictions and Dreams." ASPA News & Views, vol. 24 (January 1974).

Goode, William J. "The Protection of the Inept." <u>American Sociological Review</u>, vol. 32 (February 1967).

Gouldner, Alvin W. "Cosmopolitans and Locals: Toward an Analysis of Latent Social Roles--I." <u>Administrative Science Quarterly</u>, vol. 2 (December 1957).

Graham, George A. "Ethical Guidelines for Public Administrators: Observations on Rules of the Game." <u>Public Administration Review</u>, vol. 34 (January-February 1974).

Grimes, Andrew J., and Philip K. Berger. "Cosmopolitan-Local: Evaluation of a Construct." <u>Administrative Science Quarterly</u>, vol. 15 (December 1970).

Hampton, Robert. "Conversation with the Chairman." <u>Civil Service Journal</u>, vol. 9 (April-June 1969).

Harvey, Jerry B., and D. Richard Albertson. "Neurotic Organizations: Symptoms, Causes and Treatment." <u>Personnel Journal</u>, vol. 50 (September 1971).

Hastings, Donald W., and Glenn M. Vernon. "Ambiguous Language as a Strategy for Individual Action." Journal of Applied Behavioral Science, vol. 7 (May-June 1971).

Herzberg, Frederick. "One More Time: How Do You Motivate Employees?" Harvard Business Review, vol. 46 (January-February 1968).

Kaufman, Herbert. "Emerging Conflicts in the Doctrines of Public Administration." American Political Science Review, vol. 50 (December 1956).

_____. "Administrative Decentralization and Political Powers." Public Administration Review, vol. 29 (January-February 1969).

Kelly, Joe. "Make Conflict Work for You." Harvard Business Review, vol. 48 (July-August 1970).

Key, V. O., Jr. "Police Graft." American Journal of Sociology, vol. 40 (March 1935).

Kleber, Thomas P. "The Six Hardest Areas to Manage by Objectives." Personnel Journal, vol. 51 (August 1972).

Lake, Anthony. "Lying Around Washington." Foreign Policy, no. 2 (Spring 1971).

McConkey, Dale D. "Applying Management by Objectives to Non-Profit Organizations." S.A.M. Advanced Management Journal, vol. 38 (January 1973).

McGregor, Douglas. "An Uneasy Look at Performance Appraisal." Harvard Business Review, vol. 50 (September-October 1972).

McCormick, Ernest J., Paul R. Jeanneret, and Robert C. Mecham. "A Study of Job Characteristics and Job Dimensions as Based on the Position Analysis Questionnaire." Journal of Applied Psychology Monograph, vol. 56 (August 1972).

Merelman, Richard M. "Learning and Legitimacy." American Political Science Review, vol. 60 (1966).

Miewald, Robert D. "On Teaching Public Personnel Administration--A Weberian Perspective." Western Political Quarterly, vol. 26 (March 1973).

"Minnesota: A State That Works." _Time_, August 13, 1973.

Moynihan, Daniel P. "The Private Government of Organized Crime." _Reporter_, vol. 25 (July 6, 1961).

Murphy, Lionel V. "The First Federal Civil Service Commission: 1871-1875." _Public Personnel Review_, vol. 3 (October 1942).

Mustafa, Husain, and Anthony A. Salomone. "Administrative Circumvention of Public Policy." _Midwest Review of Public Administration_, vol. 5, no. 1 (1971).

Myers, M. Scott. "Overcoming Union Opposition to Job Enrichment." _Harvard Business Review_, vol. 49 (May-June 1971).

Patten, Thomas H., Jr. "Personnel Administration and the Will to Manage." _Human Resources Management_, vol. 11 (Fall 1972).

Patterson, Samuel C. "The Political Culture of the American States." Journal of Politics, vol. 30 (February 1968).

Rosenau, James N. "Public Protest, Political Leadership and Diplomatic Strategy." _Orbis_, vol. 14 (Fall 1970).

Ruch, Floyd L. "The Impact on Employment Procedures of the Supreme Court Decision in the Duke Power Case." _Personnel Journal_, vol. 50 (October 1971).

Rutstein, Jacob J. "Survey of Current Personnel Systems in State and Local Governments." _Good Government_, vol. 87 (Spring 1971).

Savas, E. S., and Sigmund G. Ginsburg. "The Civil Service: A Meritless System." _Public Interest_, no. 32 (Summer 1973).

Sayre, Wallace. "The Triumph of Techniques over Purpose." _Public Administration Review_, vol. 8 (Spring 1948).

Schein, Edgar H., and Gorden L. Lippitt. "Supervisory Attitudes Toward the Legitimacy of Influencing Subordinates." _Journal of Applied Behavioral Science_, vol. 2 (April/May/June 1966).

Sharkansky, Ira. "The Utility of Elazar's Political Culture: A Research Note." Polity, vol. 2 (Fall 1969).

Stahl, O. Glenn. "What the Personnel Function Is All About." Civil Service Journal, vol. 12 (July-September 1971).

Sweeney, Stephen M. "Squaw-Man in the Personnel Department." Personnel Journal, vol. 51 (December 1972).

Trice, Harrison M., James Belasco, and Joseph A. Allutto. "The Role of Ceremonials in Organizational Behavior." Industrial and Labor Relations Review, vol. 23 (October 1969).

Van Riper, Paul P. "Public Personnel Literature: The Last Decade." Public Personnel Review, vol. 22 (October 1961).

Volante, Elena M. "Are Personnel People Functioning as Tinkerers or Professionals?" Management of Personnel Quarterly, vol. 4 (Summer 1965).

Whatley, Arthur, and Larry Schieffer. "Therapeutic Relationships in Management: Thesis or Antithesis to Management Success?" S.A.M. Advanced Management Journal, 38 (January 1973).

Wilmers, Robert G., and William F. Reilly. "Decay in New York's Civil Service." New Republic, November 10, 1973.

Wilson, V. Seymour. "The Relationship Between Scientific Management and Personnel Policy in North American Administrative Systems." Public Administration, vol. 51 (Summer 1973).

Wolfinger, Raymond E., and John Osgood Field. "Political Ethos and the Structure of City Government." American Political Science Review, vol. 60 (June 1966).

Wood, Robert C. "Ethics in Government as a Problem in Executive Management." Public Administration Review, vol. 15 (Winter 1955).

Wright, Robert. "Managing Man as a Capital Asset." Personnel Journal, vol. 49 (April 1970).

Veteran's Preference Act of
1944, 48

Wall Street Journal, 86
"war on poverty," 30
Washington Post, 69, 109
Watergate, 69, 84, 151
Weber, Max, 10
Western Electric Co., 78
Wickersham Commission, 97

Wilson, James Q., 127
Wilson, Woodrow, 24, 45
Wolkomir, Nathan, 111
Wood, Robert C., 98
World War I, 24
World War II, 5, 23, 52

"zone of indifference," 111-
113

ABOUT THE AUTHOR

JAY M. SHAFRITZ, as an Assistant Professor of Political Science at Rensselaer Polytechnic Institute, holds a joint appointment in the School of Management and the Department of History and Political Science. While on leave during the 1972-73 academic year, he was a National Association of Schools of Public Affairs and Administration (NASPAA) Public Administration Fellow with the Office of Personnel of the U.S. Department of Housing and Urban Development. Previously, he was on the staff of the Personnel Department of the city of Philadelphia, the Community Renewal Program of the City Planning Commission of New York, and the Office of the Managing Director of the city of Philadelphia.

Professor Shafritz is the author of <u>Position Classification: A Behavioral Analysis for the Public Service</u> (New York: Praeger, 1973) and various articles in the personnel field. He has an M.P.A. from the Baruch College of the City University of New York and a Ph.D. in political science from Temple University.

POSITION CLASSIFICATION: A Behavioral Analysis for the Public Service
                    Jay M. Shafritz

PUBLIC SERVICE EMPLOYMENT: An Analysis of Its History, Problems, and Prospects
                    edited by Alan Gartner,
                    Russell A. Nixon and
                    Frank Riessman

THE SCOPE OF BARGAINING IN PUBLIC EMPLOYMENT
                    Joan Weitzman

MUNICIPAL LABOR RELATIONS IN NEW YORK CITY: Lessons of the Lindsay-Wagner Years
                    Raymond D. Horton

INTERNATIONAL MANUAL ON COLLECTIVE BARGAINING FOR PUBLIC EMPLOYEES
                    edited by Seymour P. Kaye and
                    Arthur Marsh

MANAGING MULTINATIONAL CORPORATIONS
                    Arvind V. Phatak

HOTEL SECURITY MANAGEMENT
                    Harvey Burstein

AFRICAN MANAGEMENT PRACTICES: Comparative Studies of Management Attitudes and Worker Perception
                    Ukandi G. Damachi